The Grimoire of Lady Sheba

Lady Sheba inherited her practice of Witchcraft from more than four generations of witches. Recognizing a profound need for a new understanding of the forces of nature, she elected to publish her grimoire, a personal magickal workbook copied by hand from the time of her initiation.

- The Power—description of the rules and requirements for correct, effective use of witchcraft
- The Tools—how to make, consecrate and use magickal instruments
- The Language—includes diagrams of the lost Theban script and Runic alphabet
- The Rituals—complete instructions for performing rituals for every purpose
- The Recipes—the famous secret herbal lore of Witchcraft, including ointments, teas, incense, perfumes, and oils
- The Dances—traditional square dances as well as magickal "witches' rounds"
- The Book of Shadows—the Holy Book of Witchcraft
- The Eightfold Path, describing the steps to magickal attainment.

First published in 1972, this ground-breaking volume includes essential information for the practicing Wiccan.

About the Author

Jessie Wicker Bell (Lady Sheba) was born in Kentucky in 1920. A modern witch, she is also a mother and grandmother. In 1971 she founded The American Order of The Brotherhood of the Wicca, and in that year her *Book of Shadows* was published, followed by *The Grimoire of Lady Sheba* in 1972, and *Witch* in 1973. She traveled, made public appearances, and lectured for a time, but left public life in the mid-1970s to care for her husband throughout a lengthy illness. Since his death she has lived quietly in retirement.

To Write to the Author

If you wish to contact the author or would like more information about this book, please write to the author in care of Llewellyn Worldwide and we will forward your request. Both the author and publisher appreciate hearing from you and learning of your enjoyment of this book and how it has helped you. Llewellyn Worldwide cannot guarantee that every letter written to the author can be answered, but all will be forwarded. Please write to:

Lady Sheba
℅ Llewellyn Worldwide
P.O. Box 64383, Dept. 0-87542-076-1
St. Paul, MN 55164-0383, U.S.A.
Please enclose a self-addressed stamped envelope for reply,
or $1.00 to cover costs. If outside U.S.A., enclose
international postal reply coupon.

Many of Llewellyn's authors have websites with additional information and resources. For more information, please visit our website at http://www.llewellyn.com. For Lllewllyn's free full-color catalog, write to *New Worlds* at the above address, or telephone 1-800-THE MOON.

Lady Sheba

Owner's Personal Record

This book belongs to_____

Birthdate _____Time_____

Place _____Long. & Lat._____

Zodiac Sign_____

Ruling Planet or Planets_____

Astral Color_____

Colors of Harmony_____

Birthstone_____

Jewels to wear for:

    Luck _____

    Health_____

    Fortune_____

Dates of great importance_____

_____

_____

Education_____

Degrees _____

Hobbies or special interest_____

_____

Dates of special events_____

_____

_____

_____

If you become a High Priest or Priestess you may keep a Coven Record of all the people you teach and also of all your Coveners.

THE
GRIMOIRE
OF
LADY
SHEBA

INCLUDES

THE BOOK OF SHADOWS

Foreword by Carl Llewellyn Weschcke

2001
Llewellyn Publications
St. Paul, Minnesota, 55164-0383, U.S.A.

FIRST EDITION, 1972
SECOND REVISED EDITION, 1974
LLEWELLYN'S CENTENNIAL EDITION, 2001
Second Printing, 2001

Book design and editing by Connie Hill
Cover design by Lisa Novak
Interior art and diagrams by Lisa Novak

Library of Congress Cataloging-in-Publication Data
Bell, Jessie Wicker
  The Grimoire of Lady Sheba / Jessie Wicker Bell
    p. cm.

  ISBN 0-87542-076-1, Hardcover

Llewellyn Publications
A Division of Llewellyn Worldwide, Ltd.
P.O. Box 64383, Dept. 0-87542-076-1
St. Paul, MN 55164-0383, U.S.A.
www.llewellyn.com

  Printed in Canada

AN IT HARM NONE

DO WHAT YE WILL.

Ancient Wiccan Rede

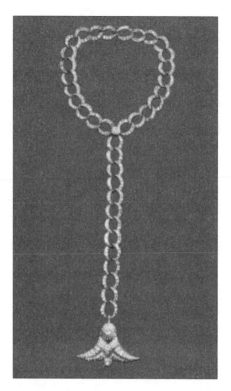

Lady Sheba's Witch Queen Necklace. The necklace is named "The Moon Goddess"; its age is unknown. Legend states that its possessor is the Queen, by birth the true and legal heir to the title of "Queen of Camelot, Camelot Coven—since the days of King Arthur." The Legend further states that should the Necklace come into possession of an unlawful queen, it would choke her to death. The Moon Goddess Necklace is a sacred talisman of the Gracious Moon Goddess, Mother of Gods and Men, Queen of Heaven and of the Universe. This is the first time that the existence of the necklace has been made public. Lady Sheba states: "I believe that the entire world of the Wise Ones have a right to know that it is still with us; it is our Holy Talisman of Our Gracious Goddess, it is our Badge of Authority." For a Witch or Warlock to be granted the privilege of simply touching the great Horns of Power, or the Diadem between the Horns, of the Moon Goddess, is the epitome of privileges within the Craft.

1, Jessie, daughter of Della, daughter of Margarett, daughter of Nancy (Nanshee) the Cherokee, have kept the Wisdom that came from the Watchers so that all who come after me may find joy and peace in the worship of the old Gods and the Gracious Goddess of the ancient Wicca.

At my physical death on this earth plane, my daughters Sandra Sue Osborn Jones and her sister Patricia Ann Osborn Jones will be anointed as the guiding force in my family descendants. This is the line of faith from Mother to daughters.

May the Holy Mother bear me witness.

Blessed Be.
Lady Sheba
Jessie Wicker Bell

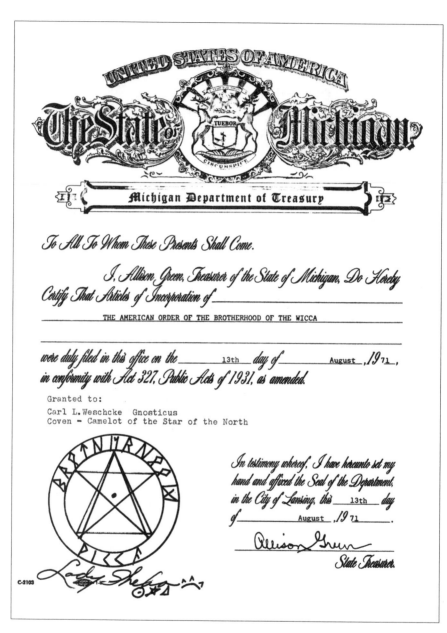

UNITED STATES OF AMERICA

The State of Michigan

Michigan Department of Treasury

To All To Whom These Presents Shall Come.

I, Allison Green, Treasurer of the State of Michigan, Do Hereby Certify That Articles of Incorporation of _____

THE AMERICAN ORDER OF THE BROTHERHOOD OF THE WICCA

were duly filed in this office on the ____ 13th ____ day of ____ August , 19 71 , in conformity with Act 327, Public Acts of 1931, as amended.

Granted to:
Carl L. Weschcke Gnosticus
Coven - Camelot of the Star of the North

In testimony whereof, I have hereunto set my hand and affixed the Seal of the Department, in the City of Lansing, this ____ 13th ____ day of ____ August , 19 71 ____ .

Allison Green
State Treasurer.

C-2103

The Charter of The American Order of the Brotherhood of the Wicca was granted to Lady Sheba on August 13, 1971. This document, bearing Lady Sheba's seal, established the Gnosticus Coven of Camelot of the Star of the North.

Contents

A Wiccan Invocation for the Land in Which You Reside

Gracious Goddess
Come thou among us,
A boon we ask for our America.
Fill our hearts with gladness,
Cleanse our minds of all
Envy, hatred and greed.
Give us knowledge and
The Wisdom to use it.
As we walk the Ancient Pathways,
Guide our footsteps
Lest we fall by the wayside.
When we stumble, lift us up.
Let us never forget
That as we receive of Thee,
We must share with our brothers.
Gracious Goddess
Show us the way to bring peace
And prosperity to our people.
Grant to our America
Strength in peace!
Gracious Goddess
We are Thy children,
As we will it
SO SHALL IT BE.

Foreword

It is with a great deal of personal pleasure that I write this foreword to our "centennial" edition of *The Grimoire of Lady Sheba*.

Llewellyn is 100 years old at the time of this writing. Always a leader in what is now known as "New Age" publishing, we are proud to have been the first to publish Lady Sheba's *Book of Shadows* in 1971 and to have been instrumental in the re-birth of Wicca.

The Grimoire of Lady Sheba was her second book, and this is the third edition. We decided to mark its republication as the celebration of our 100th year because of the role it has played in the new Witchcraft—Craft and Religion—that we call Wicca.

What so often is forgotten is that religion, at its core, does involve magic for the simple reason that each of us, at our core, is a spark of the Divine with powers to initiate change. This recognition of the "power within" moves us from mass passivity to personal responsible action. We are co-creators and must act with knowledge and responsibility within our personal field of awareness.

Wicca restored the Goddess to Her throne. The denigration of the Feminine was the ultimate "sin" of the past age. The empowerment of Women is the keynote to the birth of a new civilization we only now barely glimpse. Today, Man and Woman, and the Masculine and Feminine within each of us, are re-joined in conscious co-creation and awareness of our role within the Natural World.

As the New Age unfolds, abuse of one another and of the environment is no longer acceptable. We have discovered our unity within the planetary consciousness and are moving into a new dimension of being.

The "Craft of the Wise" is the lesson of the Witch. To find and make the tools of magic, to work and become the Divine Within, to act with Power and Love within the three-fold Law—this was the remarkable teaching found within *The Grimoire of Lady Sheba.*
Blessed Be.

Carl Llewellyn Weschcke
May 1, 2001

Introduction

This record is kept for you, my children, and all others who come after me so that all may know whereof the Wisdom came which I give unto you.

After the "burning time" of our people by the Catholic Church, witches, for the protection of the Craft, incorporated a set of laws and a powerful rite of three initiations. A postulant had to take these initiations before being taught the full concept of the ancient wisdom. The new protection laws, together with the remnants of the old ones, are what exist today as The Law. The old laws are the Redes or Maxims. Before the times of persecution we had no oaths of initiation. The knowledge, the sacred wisdom, and how to use it, were taught within the hierarchy of the families and held as a sacred trust.

Remember always that thou art witches born and the old Gods keep watch over us. They laugh with us and at us (especially when we goof up a ritual). They love us and need our help just as we love them and invoke their aid. Remember always our ancient rede, "An it harm none, do what ye will." Be happy, for all acts of love and pleasure are as a sacrifice unto the Gods; therefore, rejoice and enjoy this life you have been given. After me, you become the Keepers of the Sacred Wisdom. For verily your children must be taught; therefore do I put my books in order, that I be not found negligent when I return unto the Gods and that you may have a written reference should you need it to work the Sacred Magick.[1]

Remember the powerful witch law, "That whatsoever Thou doest it will return unto Thee threefold." You have a God-given right to self-defense, the first instinct of all living being self-preservation.

---

1. The early spelling of the word [magick] is preferred to help differentiate between it and modern stage conjuring.

Try to keep the laws of the land in which you reside. Do your utmost to live in harmony with your neighbors. If you find you cannot, then move your household to the countryside where there is peace and communion with the Gods.

Keep your thoughts under control. "Thoughts are things, and as a man thinketh so he is."

Whenever you give your word, remember that witch law requires that "you keep your word." Your given word must not return unto you void. "Speak little and listen much." Do your sacred work alone or with the coven. Do not speak constantly of the sacred work. Remember that "power shared is power lost."

Our families have always been huntsmen and fishermen and I would remind you of the witch law of the wild kingdom: "You will take only what you need for food, no more. Thou must never waste the life of any living creature. Never kill all of the covey or the tribe. Some must be left to continue the race." Never knowingly take the life of a mother animal or fowl. If in hunting it should happen, ask forgiveness of the Gods and make use of the kill. Don't waste it.

The magnificent sacred wisdom that was given to mankind when the Watchers (Sons of God) elected to come to earth to teach man the holy mysteries has been almost all lost—first by the Flood of Noah's time, then by the destruction waged by the Christian Church.

The wisdom of the Watchers is being regained. Now is the time of mystic renaissance. Occult research has exploded across the face of the earth and man is throwing off the chains of organized religion that have shackled his mind.

Remember, there are as many pathways to God as there are the breaths of men, each human being traveling the best way he knows back to God. For there is but one Creator, one God, from which all others emanate.

The worship of the one God through the medium of the Great Horned God and the Moon Goddess is expressed by the rituals or rites of the Wicca,

There is wisdom in worship. Always remember that beyond the duality is the one from whom we came and eventually to whom we return.

It is the great return home which should be the hope of us all and uppermost in our minds as we perform our rites. The worship of the One Essence manifested in nature (moon-female, sun-male, sea-earth) is what Wicca is all about. The worship of God made manifest in nature is not idol worship.

These benevolent powers—the Watchers, Mighty Ones, Sons of Angelic Forces, planetary spirits—together with the knowledge that all Gods are one God and all Goddesses are one Goddess are the true deities of the Wicca.

SO BE IT.

1

The Power

The foundation on which all your witch power is built is the *witches' pyramid*. The first side of the four so-called sides of the pyramid is your dynamic, controlled will; the second, your imagination or the ability to see your desire accomplished; third, unshakable and absolute faith in your ability to accomplish anything you desire; and fourth, secrecy—"power shared is power lost." You and your co-workers must work in solitude, peace, and harmony.

These four things, will power, imagination, faith, and secrecy are the basic rules and the absolute basic requirements for the working of Witchcraft. Without all four working together you cannot accomplish the arts and crafts of the Wise Ones.

With your pyramid of power working for you, be sure you have ample knowledge of the universal power tides. The source and the ebb and flow of these cosmic power tides are marked by the movements of the Sun, Moon, and planets through the solar system.

The eight great solar power tides that occur throughout the year mark the time of our religious Sabbats. This is our cosmic calendar. They are a time to draw close to the Gods and receive the magical rejuvenation from contact through the cosmic power tides that are closer to the earth at the Solstices and Equinoxes.

It is not enough to know or possess knowledge and power. One must know how to focus or aim the power in the desired direction and for the purpose intended.

The famous witches' "cone of power" is accomplished by using your pyramid powers to build and focus the force or power raised by your own electric and magnetic body, and brought together and held as a beam of light (power) by your will, within the Magick Circle.

Then by the force of your will, command the power cone to come forth and accomplish the purpose for which it was raised.

The Magick Circle acts as a lens to constrain and focus the magical cone of power, very similar to the lens on a modern spotlight.

When you begin to build the cone of power and cold chills are tingling up and down your spine, and your will has increased in power and determination until you feel highly intoxicated and ready to explode; when you have experienced all these things, then know that you have succeeded in raising the mystical, magical cone of power. When you know you have succeeded, drop to the floor or earth and point your Wand in the direction you are sending the power, binding your will to the cone of power and visualizing the accomplished result.

You may also raise the cone of power and send it forth as a familiar in the form of a bird or ball of light, etc., and have it report back to you when it has completed its errand.

"If at first you don't succeed, try, try again."

The mystical magic of Witchcraft is the highest science known to man. Practical Witchcraft is the knowledge of and the ability to manipulate the metaphysical and metapsychical universal laws of nature established by the Creator of the universe, and it encompasses the lowest of the universal laws of nature, unto the highest laws of the spirit.

The powers obtained by the knowledge of and the use of Witchcraft are neither good nor evil, but are neutral. The universal laws remain the same. It is the application of the laws by the individual and the results obtained by their use that alone determines what is known as white or black Witchcraft.

The power comes from one source only—the God Force. Our God and Creator of all things did not create anything unclean or evil. but as either positive or negative. Man gave these positive and negative forces within nature the aspect of good or evil.

The universal law of "Like Unto Like" upon which the Sympathetic Magick aspect of Witchcraft is based has been used since time began.

Witchcraft is used today in America by people who would be shocked to find out that the wooden duck decoys set out on the water to attract the ducks from the sky is and always will be Witchcraft. This is a modern example of the universal law of "Like Unto Like" or "That Like Produces Like," which is often called "the Law of Similarity."

Another aspect of Sympathetic Magick is "Contact." Witches believe that things that have once been in contact with each other, such as a person's clothing containing their perspiration or things that have been once a part of the body (cut hair or nails or urine) continue to act on each other no matter what the distance between the severed parts.

Knowing Sympathetic Magick to be an application of the universal law of "Like Unto Like," we thus make use of this ancient wisdom in the rituals by using waxen images or clay puppets.

I would especially have you remember that miracles and magick acts are accomplished by the use of the powers of your mind which today's scientists cannot explain or understand.

2

The Eightfold Path

The Eightfold Path has never been published openly before. Without this knowledge you cannot work the Arts Magickal, since the Eightfold Path to the Center is the basic essential in all the workings of the Craft.

The First Path

Intention and concentration of intent. Mental imagery or visualization. Meditation.

The Second Path

Rising upon the planes. Using the many Trance States, better known today as "altered states of consciousness." Projection of the Astral Body.

The Third Path

The Keys: rites, rituals, chants, spell-casting, runes, charms, amulets, talismans, the magick link.

The Fourth Path

The correct and controlled use of drugs (hemp, kat, mushrooms, etc.), ritual wines, whiskey (known as "the elixir of life"), and incense.

The Fifth Path

The dance and kindred practices to raise the fiery cone of power.

The Sixth Path

Warricking, blood control by use of the Cords, breath control, and kindred practices.

The Seventh Path

The ancient rite of scourging to purify.

The Eighth Path

The great rite, the spiritual union as well as the physical union of male and female to create life. Sex Magick.

Comment: The five essentials for the working of the Eightfold Path are *Intention, Preparation,* the *Magick Circle, Self-purification,* and the *Consecrated Tools.*

To me the *Intention* of the Wise One is the most important feature of the Eightfold Path. You must know beyond any shadow of a doubt that you can and will succeed. This is the absolute essential of every operation of magick or religious worship.

Preparation: You must be properly prepared for the work you are doing according to the rules of the Art, and you must take note of the cosmic laws and the planetary times. All ritual preparation must be observed or you cannot work the Arts Magickal.

The *Magick Circle,* our temple between the realm of the Gods and the world of man, must be properly formed, consecrated, and purified.

Self-Purification, cleanliness of body and mind. You must be prepared and purified according to the rules of the Art. If a rite should be of long duration, lasting through a Moon and Sun, then the Circle and the operator must be purified often through the night and the day.

All of your holy altar tools must be properly constructed, puri-fied, and *consecrated* to the God/Goddess. Keep your tools highly charged with power. This can be done by recharging in the Magick Circle with the Dance, by concentration, or as I personally do, by sleeping with my Magick Knife, feeding it constantly.

There are many ways of using the Eightfold Path and the five essentials to gain the Center. The Center is the union with the God/Goddess, the source and sustainer of our being.

All of the Paths do not combine well together; but many of the Paths can be combined to bring faster and more powerful results. Each person must work out his own best combinations.

The First Path, intention and concentration of intent, is essential in all workings. It combines easily with all the other paths and leads to the Second Path, the union of the operator with the evoked Entity.

The Fourth Path is a very powerful way to the Center. The aids quickly unlock the inner eye and swiftly release the spirit from its physical prison. Therefore, "Judge Ye wisely with whom Ye will choose to tread the Pathways to Wisdom, for Ye must accompany them until they stand in the Divine Light of the Center." This knowledge must not be taught to fools.

3

The Tools

Make your own ritual accessories as far as you are able. Swords, Athames, Bollines, Chalices, Bells, Thuribles, candle holders, and Cauldrons can be obtained from any occult supply company or occult shop. Never haggle over the price of an altar object.

The holy symbols may be engraved on your tools with an ordinary engraver's pencil or you may paint them on. Consecrate and bless all ritual and altar items.

The Witches' Wand

The Wand may be made from many different woods, willow, hazel, rowan, elder, oak, and mistletoe. I made mine from the elderberry, which has a pithy center and is easy to work with.

Cut an elderberry limb about one inch in diameter and the length from your elbow to the tip of your forefinger. Remove the bark and smooth with fine sandpaper. Remove about two inches of the pith inside the wood. Take enough cotton to fill the space and prick your thumb with a new needle, letting from three to five drops of blood fall on the cotton. Load your Wand with the cotton in the space where you removed the pith. Seal with dripping wax from the altar candle. Paint or engrave a Pentagram and your witch name on the opposite end of the Wand from the cotton. Wax and polish the entire Wand, then consecrate with Water, Fire, Wine, Oil, and three deep breaths of Air. These represent the four elements. Do this in the names of Arida and Kernunnos. Your magick Wand is now ready to do your will.

Comment: The most important aid in Witchcraft is your Wand.

The Markings on the Tools

Athame and Sword: Top side—carve initial of witch name and:

| The Eight-fold Path to the Center | The Arrow of Magic Issuing Forth | The Perfect Couple |

Underside—carve the following:

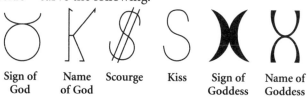

| Sign of God | Name of God | Scourge | Kiss | Sign of Goddess | Name of Goddess |

Bolline: Top side handle—carve the following:

Top side blade—carve the following:

Underside handle—carve the following:

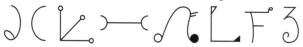

Scourge: Carve witch degree initials as acquired:

| First Degree | Second Degree | Third Degree |

Cup: Carve a pentacle and a crescent Moon.

Wand: Carve witch name and a pentacle.

The Athame

With the Athame or Sword in your hand you are absolute ruler of the Magick Circle. These tools are used to perform all magical rites. They are used to subdue and punish rebellious spirits, demons, and evil genii.

The Bolline

The witches' white-handled knife is used to make instruments, cut Pentagrams on candles, etc. It can only be used inside the Magick Circle.

The Stang

This is a straight piece of rowan wood (mountain ash) with a fork at one end, used in ancient times as a staff. A shorter version is used to beat out the rhythm of the circle dances.

Altar

Any consecrated place or thing used to hold the ritual instruments used in the Magick Circle.

Cauldron

A kettle, usually of iron, or an ordinary cooker in which food or drink is prepared over the Balefire for the rites.

Cord

The magick binding Cord is made from strands of red wool or ribbon. It is plaited (braided) with a loop tied at one end to represent the female aspect. The other end is left frayed to represent the male aspect. Measure your binding Cord around your head and loop a knot, continue around your chest, loop a knot, around your waist, loop a knot, around your hips, loop a knot, around your knees, loop a knot, around your feet, knot. The finished Cord should measure nine feet in length. It is worn around the waist during all rites and is used in binding spells. It is used to bind the sigils of the art, the material basis, and is necessary to enforce your will. Tie your Cord around you by passing the male end through the loop (female) and secure.

Necklaces

Female witches wear strings of beads representing the "circle of rebirth." The beads are made from acorns, seeds, wood, or seashells. The Witch Queen wears a black Necklace. The other coveners wear any color Necklace they like.

Witches' Besom or Broom

A witch Broom is made from six different woods: birch, willow, broom, hazel, rowan, and hawthorne. The twigs of these trees are bound to a handle (any length) by sedge grass or a long bendable twig of willow. Insert a three-inch plug of blackthorn in the top of the broom where the binding is done.

Pentacle

Made from a round piece of wood usually seven inches in diameter with a Pentagram inscribed or painted on it. It is used for the purpose of calling up the appropriate spirits.

Censer of Incense

This is used to encourage and welcome good spirits and to banish evil spirits.

Scourge

The handle is made of birch, the four thongs of leather. This instrument is a symbol of the "Power of Domination." It is also used to cause suffering and purification, for it is written, "To learn thou must suffer and be purified."

Rite to Consecrate Your Ritual Instruments

By the force of your imagination and your dynamic will power, charge your instrument, concentrating on the purpose you wish it to serve. Grasp the tool in your strongest hand and concentrate your desire into it (Desire–Will Power).

Concentrate your desire into the tool with a rock-hard, unshakable faith that it will increase in power with each new day, that the power within the tool will last as long as the tool itself, that ghosts, spirits, human beings and animals are to obey your will, that they will obey your magick tool, whether in the physical world or the astral or mental plane. Charge your instrument to work on dead material also.

Concentrate on the Akasha principle—the Life Force—and draw down this Life Force from the Universal God Force into your instrument. Remember to charge it with the idea that the Life Force power within the tool will automatically intensify from one day to the next.

Charge your tool to automatically. without any effort on your part, bring a piece of Life Force from the Universal God Force, which will then radiate from your instrument whenever and to whatever it is needed. This force in your magical tool can be used for the good of yourself and for others, as you wish. It may also be used against your enemies.

SO MOTE IT BE.

Full Moon Ceremony to Consecrate a New Wand and/or to Recharge Old Ones (Esbat)

The High Priest or High Priestess casts the Magick Circle. The High Priestess invokes the Watchers to bear witness and to bless the work being done. The High Priest arranges the Altar in the North of the circle. The High Priestess consecrates the holy water, candles, and incense. Then she purifies herself, the Circle and Altar, and the High Priest.

Each male covener is now blessed as he passes in front of her. The High Priest now takes the holy water and purifies the female coveners as they come into the circle. As they enter the Circle and are purified, they pass before the High Priestess and curtsy, saying, "Blessed Be." As the male coveners pass before her, she purifies them and they bow and say "Blessed Be" and kiss her on the right cheek.

The High Priestess faces North and assumes the Goddess Position. The coveners stand within the circle, alternately, male and female. All coveners grasp their Wands in their strongest hand and repeat the Consecration Ritual, with the High Priest and High Priestess leading.

The High Priest pours red wine into the Chalice and holds it cupped with both hands for the High Priestess to bless. She blesses the wine with the Athame and then sips from the Chalice and passes it to the High Priest, who sips from it and passes it to the coveners. The coveners sip from the cup and then it is returned to the High Priest, who returns it to the High Priestess, who drains the Chalice.

The High Priestess gives the Gods, who were invoked, license to depart and thanks them for attending and blessing the work. The Circle is now closed.

Lady Sheba in the "Osiris Risen" position.
(For the complete text of Drawing Down the Moon ritual, see pp. 167–169.)

Lady Sheba invoking the gods.

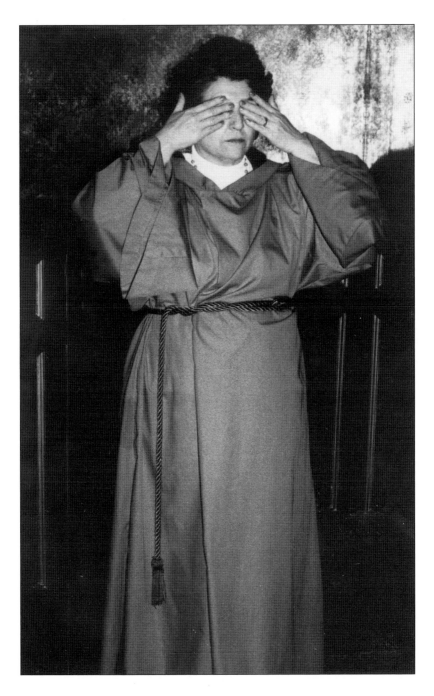

Lady Sheba's Self-Blessing Ritual—"Never search for evil!"
(For the complete text of this ritual, see pp. 38–39.)

Lady Sheba's Self-Blessing Ritual—"Never listen to gossip!"

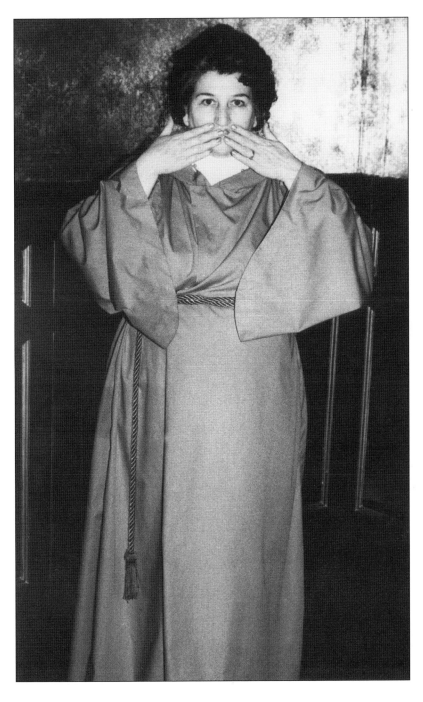

Lady Sheba's Self-Blessing Ritual—"Never give voice to evil!"

Silver Money Ritual—"Greeting the Moon."
(For the complete text of this ritual, see pp. 50–51.)

Silver Money Ritual—"Bowing to the Moon."

Silver Money Ritual—"Turning over the Silver."

Money rocks are laid out on Lady Sheba's altar. The rocks are from the sea—silver coins are laid on them to bring money. To use, one would light a green candle and ask the Holy Mother for needed wealth. Lady Sheba keeps the rocks on her altar to assist with prayers for a family member.

Lady Sheba's magic cards, laid out on her holy table. The cards were blessed by the Holy Mother, and some of them marked as a gift to Lady Sheba.

Lady Sheba's altar is set up before a zodiac wheel wall hanging. The Holy Mother (Goddess) statue shines at the center of the altar, her place of honor. The Buddha is placed at her feet with her bell to the left. The fish figure at the right is draped with jewelry for health and wealth; a dream of fish means money.

Lady Sheba's magic broom, sword, and scourge hang beside her altar.

The wall hanging on the left, a very old, magickal piece, is rich in symbolism, and features a secret pocket. On the right is a closeup view of a magickal wand, and in front of it is a cut-glass holy water chalice. The chalice has never been used for any other purpose, and has never been empty. The Holy Mother came to Lady Sheba, put her hand in the chalice, and blessed it.

4

The Language

In the beginning the Wicca had their own language. We still have our own ancient Runic alphabet, but very little remains of our old language.

During the times of persecution, the Wiccan people were afraid to speak their true language, therefore it became a lost tongue.

The Runic alphabet is ours; don't let any school teacher ever make you believe otherwise. During the course of your school years you will hear much speculation from scholars and theologians about the Runes. HEED THEM NOT. It always has been and always will be the magical, sacred alphabet of the witches.

I urge you to learn to write the Runes. It is good to keep your Book of Shadows in our ancient Holy Script.

The Alphabet

Theban Script: The Wiccan alphabet and writing to be used.

𝒜	ℬ	𝒞	𝒟	ℰ	ℱ
A	B	C	D	E	F

G	H	I	K	L	M

N	O	P	Q	R	S

T	V	Y	Z

Note: Letters of confusion are inserted anywhere to confuse the curious as follows:

The Runic Alphabet (alternative script).

ᚠ	ᛒ	ᛃ	ᛠ	ᛗ	ᚡ
A	B	C	D	E	F
ᚷ	ᚺ	ᛁ	ᛎ	ᚲ	ᚱ
G	H	I	J	K	L
ᛗ	ᛏ	◇	ᛦ	ᚹ	◹
M	N	Ng	O	P	Q
ᚱ	ᛀ	↑	ᚦ	ᚢ	⌐V
R	S	T	Th	U	V
ᚦ	ᚷ	ᛃ	ᛉ		
W	X	Y	Z		

Remnants of the Witches' Language

Alrum—Talisman of rowanwood

Amulet—Object to bring luck to bearer

Ardane—Equivalent of ordain

Athame—Witches' black-handled knife

Baculum—Wand

Baile—A dance

Balefire—Ritual fire

Bolline—Witches' white-handled knife

Ban—To curse

Bane—Poison herb

Banshee—A guardian family spirit that forewarns of coming death in the family

Barrow—Burial ground

Beltane—Walpurgis, June 21, Sabbat

Besom—Broom

Bound—The result of using a binding Cord

Brile—To roast meat on a sharpened stick over an open fire

Britches—Pants

Candlemas—February 2, religious Sabbat

Charm—Words of magick or talisman

Cingulum—Witches' magick Cord

Civer—A quilt, blanket, bedspread

Clog—The Runic staff wand

Clog Almanac—A notch stick or primitive calendar made by cutting notches on the four sides of the clog

Conjur—To summon a spirit

Coven—Twelve members and a High Priest and a High Priestess

Covener—A witch; member of a coven

Covenstead—The territory ruled by a High Priest or a High Priestess

Cowan—Uninvited, uninitiated guest

Dagycle—Witches' image needle

Deosil—Clockwise, follow the sun

Dolmen—Circle of stones, used as the Magick Circle

Dwale—Deadly nightshade

Elements—The four elements—Water, Fire, Earth, and Air; the basic manifestation of matter

Elffire—Need fire, wild fire, the flame produced by the drawing down of a spark of elemental fire from the Universal Force to light the Balefire

Elven—Elvenfold, descendants of the Watchers

Esbat—Full Moon ceremony

Evoke—Conjure

Familiar—Elemental servant

Farce—Untrue or false commitment

Fatch —Something accomplished by means of a fetch

Fetch—Wraith, a witches' familiar

Futhark—The Runic alphabet of the witches

Ganch—A wound made by a boar's tusk; also to execute by impaling on a stake or hook

Grimoire—Witches' personal workbook, a book of spells

Haft—A dagger

Hag—A bitter, hateful woman

Haggle—To argue

Hagride—To torment by Witchcraft

Hairyfoot—A poison mushroom connected with fairy rings

Halch—To knot, tie, or embrace

Halcyon—The twice seven (fourteen) days of tranquillity, traditionally occurring, at the Winter Solstice (Yule)

Halloween—October 31, religious Sabbat

Handmaiden—Young girl witch

Harpy—An elemental created to torment another person. Also malicious mothers-in-law

Havelock—The binding of a person by giving them a covering for their head (headscarf, cap)

Hearthrock—The stone before the fireplace

Hoc—Trouble

Knot—Runic knot, a form of interlaced ornament used on jewels, swords, tools, called the witches' knot

Lady—High Priestess

Lammas—August 1, religious Sabbat

Ligature—A preventive form of binding with the Cord

Magic—The use of the ancient wisdom of the Watchers

Magus—Wizard, warlock

Pact—Signed pledge of silence

Palet—A quilt or blanket being used as a temporary place to sleep

Patchouli—Graveyard dust, also an herb

Pooka—A mischievous, helpful, lovable elemental spirit

Rede—A witch law or maxim

Runes—Witches' alphabet

Seeing Stone—Crystal ball

Shade—Spirit of a dead human

Siderite—A lodestone charm

Sigil—The seal or signature of a spirit

Simple—Tea

Tag Lock—Lock of victims hair, used in spells

Talisman—Consecrated power object

Thing—Ward of confusion used as a substitute name for a person, place, or "thing"

Thurible—Incense burner

Vampire—Predatory fetch

Warrik—Garrot, rope, girth

Werewolf—Fetch in wolf form

Widdershins—Anticlockwise [counterclockwise]

Wraith—Projected astral body of a witch ensouled with her consciousness

Common Witch Phrases

I'll fetch it—to obtain by using a fetch

They're bound to do it—a person cannot stop a happening because a spell has been cast to cause a definite performance

Keep your Hearthrock clean—a witch must by law keep a clean house

To be in Hoc—to be in trouble

I was fatched over—being summoned by a fetch

Shet the door—shut the door

I'm gonna boggle his mind—influence another's mind by Witchcraft

Don't gerit too tight—don't bind a fellow human too much

He's a Lupe in a Ram's coat—a person who cannot be trusted

A Lupe is loose—a traitor is in the neighborhood

Danger is never overcome without danger—a witch maxim

A slave works with his hands—a witch uses his mind (maxim)

Who will brile the meat—who will do the work

Kicking the wind—being hanged

Beware the Tempter—a false person

A wild boar can be held at bay by a small dog—a maxim

Burning Britches—a beating, also passion

Animals have feet, not hands—do not expect too much from beasts of burden

He's a trifling man—lazy man

Allus faithful—trustworthy

A friend in need, is a friend indeed—a maxim

You can't change the past, but you can do something about the future—a maxim

Like a thief in the night—sneaking

Seek your enemy in secret—a maxim

The stupid fear luck, the wise endure it—a maxim

Keep your mouth shet—Be silent—a maxim

They who live in glass castles, ought not to throw stones—a maxim

No lamb wants to be chased by a wolf—a maxim

Bare not your head to the midday sun—a maxim

Three things are the God-given right of every man—*his woman, his whiskey, and the right to choose his own master*—a maxim

The Laws sometimes sleep but they never die—a maxim

He's a littern—a modern litterbug

No one person can do everything—a maxim

Cutting a caper—being drunk

Frying Flitters—frying pancakes

A Loady—a stool-pigeon

Stirring up a hornets' nest—gossiping with the intent to cause trouble

To fashion—to mold or to make

Better late than never—a maxim

A Wiccan Grace

Mother!
Darksome and Divine
Bless my food,
Bless my wine.
Give me Health,
Wealth, and Wisdom,
The Divine Three.
And as I WILL!
SO MOTE IT BE!

Sourabaddio: Ode to the Moon

The Moon hath laid her light in this fair place.
There lingers well the dewy Rose,
She lays her petals to the Earth,
And all the world
Sleeps in silent contemplation.
O Sourahaddio, Sourahaddio.
Thou art not so deniably unerring
That thou cans't not yet turn thy face,
Thy lovely face,
Towards the Denizens of this Earth.
Give us thy peace,
That we may be at one with Thee.

Comment: This was a gift from a sea witch to an English witch to me.

5

The Rituals

My beloved children,

In these following pages I am giving you the rites, rituals, and spells that I love most. They are ancient and powerful and I think they are beautiful. For many aeons past they have brought joy to the Wicca. Now I give them to the world, that all mankind may know the beauty of the ancient rites.

Lady Sheba

To Make a Ritual Work

1. You must know and control your witches' pyramid.

2. Know the correct phase of the Moon.

3. Know the right day of the week.

4. Know the correct hour of the day.

5. Know the ruling deity and how to invoke his influence or power for the work you intend to do.

6. If the rite is a Jupiter, Mars, or Saturn rite, then you must know the correct planetary hour.

To Cast a Spell

Cast your Magick Circle and purify yourself and your Circle with holy water. Invoke the Watchers to bear witness. With a pen and Dragon's Blood write your desire on a red candle. Light the candle and burn the incense. In a clear and commanding voice repeat this spell:

> *Upon this Candle I will write,*
> *What I receive of thee this night.*
> *Grant what I wish you to do,*
> *I dedicate this rite to you.*
> *I trust that you will grant this boon,*
> *O Lovely Goddess of the Moon.*
> *I call Earth to bond my Spell,*
> *Air speed its travel well,*
> *Fire give it spirit from above,*
> *Water quench my spell with love.*
> *SO MOTE IT BE.*

Comment: I dearly love this powerful spell.

The Lore of the Waxen Image

The use of the image in occult practice goes back in time to prehistoric Imitative or Sympathetic Magick, where an image of clay was used.

The methods employed through the ages have varied in effectiveness, but if used properly, it can be safely stated that the desired result can be attained in a number of cases that will consistently outweigh chance.

Before using the image, please note that we advocate using it strictly for operations of White Magick.

This image should be used primarily as a focal point, much in the same way that a crystal ball is used by the fortuneteller. Since the image becomes an effect, a sacrifice to the magical operation, always use a new image for each desired effect!

To Create an Elemental or Witches' Familiar

This is only one of the many ways to create an Elemental or Witches' Familiar. Sometimes it takes a lot of practice; but it is worthwhile and you will be rewarded mightily for the work and willpower you put into learning how to create and control an Elemental.

I am going to give you this ritual in step-by-step instructions, so that you can't possibly fail. Remember it takes willpower and practice. It can be done, and exactly as I tell you to do it.

Step 1: Light a candle and incense, and in peace and quiet, meditate until you are at ease.

Step 2: Start chanting in your mind exactly what you wish to accomplish.

Step 3: Narrow your thinking and chanting down to one phrase that you can issue as a command. Keep repeating this one phrase in chant form.

Step 4: Now you are ready to create your Familiar or Elemental. Hold your hands about six inches apart, with your palms slightly cupped and facing each other.

Step 5: Imagine a triangle of energy radiating from your forehead and your heart to a point between your palms. You can also imagine a pyramid of power, the sides of the pyramid taking in all of the head and chest area; or if you are into Sex Magick, picture a whirling cone of power, rising from the genital area and gaining strength as it rises upward through the power lines of your body and is focused from the mind and sent out.

Step 6: Call upon the Gracious Goddess or Horned God to give life to this Elemental that is being created between your palms. Thank them for their help. You can now feel this Elemental grow. As you breathe, let your palms move slightly back and forth toward each other, in a pulsating motion in rhythm with your breathing.

Step 7: Breathe in and out (also moving your hands) until the Elemental becomes a swirling ball of energy between your palms. All this time remember to keep up your mental chant of the one-line command. Keep the vision of the Triangle of Power (energy) flowing from your forehead and your heart to the form within your palms. If you are using the Pyramid or Sex Magick, do the same with these two paths.

Step 8: Now breathe right into the Elemental Form the very breath of life. From the Goddess or God within yourself give life unto your creation.

Step 9: At this point you may find that you are in an altered state of consciousness or in a light state of trance. Now rise to your feet and command the Elemental to go forth and fulfill its mission and serve you well. Surround it with a mental circle of protection and throw it into the air. Spread your arms wide in the ancient Pentagram position (the Goddess position). Repeat your one-line command, ending:

> *So be it done*
> *Three, six, nine, twenty-one,*
> *End Ye well what here's begun!*

Ancient Seven-Day Wish

Light a seven-knobbed candle. Burn one knob each day at the same hour of the day. As you concentrate and stare into the candle flame, focus your mind on your wish. Allow no other thought to intrude.

Use a colored candle corresponding to the nature of the wish. Don't forget to chart the right phase of the Moon and the right planetary time for spirit influence before you light the candle to begin the spell.

Love Magick

Materials needed: One new candle, two new bowls, clean water for filling one bowl, and fresh crumbly earth for the other bowl.

First, procure a lock of hair, fingernail clippings, or a tiny piece of material from the soiled clothing of the person whom you wish to love you. Write the loved one's name on a piece or small scrap of new paper on the first night of the Waxing Moon, being sure to have the Moon over the left shoulder.

Place the bowl of earth on the left side, then place the bowl of water next to the bowl of earth, and lastly, place the candle next to the water and light the candle.

Then, holding the image in the left hand, mentally transpose the image of the loved one's face onto the face of the waxen image, so that, by the force of your will and imagination, the image actually becomes the person whom you wish to affect with your desires. Then, taking one of the thorns in your right hand, slowly pierce the forehead of the image and say:

> *As I pierce the brain of* (name) *with this thorn, let him or her be overcome with loving thoughts of me.*

Then bring the image close to your mouth and breathe upon it three times. Hold it to the East, saying:

> *O Ye Mighty Ones of the East, know my desire and bless me with success in the name of Uriel, Blessed Be.*

Then hold it North, saying:

> *O Ye Mighty Ones of the North, know my desire and bless me with success in the name of Uriel, Blessed Be.*

Now take the image and place it in the bowl of water briefly, and then hold it up to the West saying:

> *O Ye Mighty Ones of the West, know my desire and bless me with success in the name of Gabriel, Blessed Be.*

Next, take the image and pass it over the flame of the candle, and while holding it up to the South say:

> *O Ye Mighty Ones of the South, know my desire*
> *and bless me with success in the name of Michael,*
> *Blessed Be.*

After this bury the doll with the thorns intact. Then, add the earth to the water and douse the candle in the mixture; breathe three times on the resulting concoction. After this, pour it on the buried doll and say:

> *May this all come to pass in the name of the Great*
> *Mother and the Mighty Dead, Yod He Vau He, by*
> *the Ancient Ones, Blessed Be.*

The operation is then complete and should be considered to be in the capable hands of the Ancient Ones. The desired effect should be accomplished by the time the Moon is full.

Healing Magick

The same materials are used as in the former operation; this ritual should also be performed on the first night of the Waxing Moon.

The name of the person should be written on a new scrap of paper and placed with nail clippings, a drop of blood, if possible, and a lock of the afflicted person's hair. If these are impossible to obtain, the person's name on the small scrap of paper will be sufficient.

More than one person can participate in this operation. All persons just use their combined will and imagination to impress mentally the image of the ill person and to load the image with the positive healing power of the elements in the following manner.

Place the candle, bowl of water, and bowl of earth in a row as was done in the previous Love Magick operation. Then pierce the image with a thorn into the area of the image corresponding to the afflicted part of the person whom you wish to heal, saying these words:

> *Let this thorn carry to the afflicted part of the body*
> *of* (name) *the blessed healing power of the four*

elements, enforced by the combined wills of all
gathered here. We all humbly ask the blessing of
the Ancient Ones, Yod He Vau He, Blessed Be.

Then go through the same steps to charge the image with the healing properties of the elements as stated in the love magick ritual, only right before the doll is buried the thorn is removed and burned as you say:

Thus shall the evil within you be destroyed, in the
name of the Ancient Ones, Blessed Be.

Fertility Magick

This ritual is performed on the eve of the Spring Equinox, March 21, and is accomplished in the following manner.

A female waxen image and a male waxen image are both used for this ceremony, which is enacted to insure a bountiful harvest.

The two images are bound together crosswise, using green thread, with genitals touching. Then, as previously mentioned, the bowls of water and earth, along with a new candle, are set in a row before the bound images. You must then lift the images to the lips and breathe upon them three times, saying:

May the Ancient Ones of the East make their
mating bountiful, and smile upon them with love
and blessedness. Be Ye then fruitful in union. Yod
He Vau He, Blessed Be.

Then sprinkle the images with earth and repeat the previous benediction, substituting "Ancient Ones of the West." After this, pass the figures over the candle flame and repeat the benediction, substituting "Ancient Ones of the South."

Then bury the figure in the earth. Mix the earth from the bowl into the bowl of water and douse the flame in the mixture. When that is accomplished, lift the mixture and breathe upon it, saying:

Blessed Be this union of the elements. Bountiful be
under the eyes of the Great Mother. Fruitful be all

> *things in their cycle. This we ask in the name of the*
> *Ancient Ones. Yod He Vau He, Blessed Be.*

Then pour the mixture over the buried figures and depart reverently.

These are but a few examples of the ceremonies which can be performed with the waxen images. Volumes could be written concerning the various rituals which have been used through the ages with images of this type, but the brief account we have given will surely suggest numerous methods in which the images can be employed, using the basic element-loading ritual that we have employed in the examples given.

An Ancient Sacrificial Rite

Time: Celebrate this rite at the Full Moon preceding the Vernal Equinox or Easter Sunday morning.

Place: To be celebrated in the open air, underneath the sky. Use your backyard, city park, or seashore.

This rite was given to me on the spiritual plane by the Gracious Goddess. The Goddess did accompany me to a beautiful wood and stood by my side and instructed me as I performed this beautiful ritual. in the words of the Goddess: "If you give four eggs unto the Gods, you will receive three eggs in return for each egg you give." I asked why I had four eggs to keep while others around me had only one and she said: "Because you are a High Priestess." Then she told me this sacrifice was where the modern custom of coloring eggs at Easter came from.

The Rite: Build your fire on the naked earth. Pour water into the Cauldron and place four small eggs and one large egg (edible fowl eggs) in the Cauldron and set the Cauldron on the fire. Put a red dye (food coloring) into the water, and boil until the eggs are hard-boiled.

Remove the eggs from the Cauldron. Write on two of the small eggs the God's name, Kernunnos, and write the Goddess's name, Arida, on the other small eggs. Arrange these eggs on a white cloth, skin, or prepare in this manner:

The four eggs should form a line, yet not touch together. The four eggs are to be kept as a perpetual sacrifice before the Gods.

The one large egg is to be taken from the shell and the names of Arida and Kernunnos written on each end of the egg. Then cut the egg in half with the cut end on the tray and the pointed ends with the Gods' names turned up. Cut the two halves each into four quarters. You now have eight quarters or pieces of egg, as shown here:

In your own words bless the four small eggs and dedicate them as a perpetual sacrifice to Arida and Kernunnos. Bless the fifth egg that has been cut as a sacrifice to be eaten by all present.

Bless the Chalice of wine and pass the egg and wine to all who have attended the rite.

Comment: This was truly one of the most beautiful and rewarding experiences of my life. To know that the Gracious Goddess chose to reveal to mankind, through me, this ancient and holy rite, fills me with humility and gratitude. This knowledge, once known to all the Wicca, had been lost somewhere in dark ages past. It has been returned to us by our Gracious Goddess and all the witches of the world rejoice with me.

Emergency Spell

If there should arise the need for a fast invocation, take your handkerchief or a scarf, or even a sock from your foot. Brush the space where you stand, then drop your magic binding Cord down around your feet in a circle.

Turn your face toward the North and invoke the Watchers. Then invoke to the East, South, and to the West. If you are constrained and dare not speak aloud, invoke the Watchers mentally, using your mind power. Mentally or aloud state your request (boon) to the Gracious Goddess. Be dynamic and very sure of what you want. In your mind literally scream the words that follow.

> *As I say,*
> *So mote it be,*
> *As I will,*
> *It shall be done!*
> *Blessed Be.*

Then dismiss the Watchers of the North, East, South, and West and thank them for bearing witness. Pick up your Cord. It is done.

The Fisherman's Spell

Cast your Magick Circle. Purify yourself, the Circle, and Altar. Invoke the Gods to bear witness to the work being done. Light candles and incense. Make an image of a swimming fish and sprinkle it with holy water and with wine from the Chalice. Pass it over the flame of the candle three times. Blow upon the fish image three warm, deep, breaths of air, saying:

> *Hear ye! Gracious Goddess, I dedicate this rite to*
> *you. Bless Thou! this sacred fish that I have fash-*
> *ioned. And ere I cast it forth into the waters of*
> (name the river, lake, or sea) *it shall draw unto my*
> *net, an abundance of fish.*

Give the Ancient Gods license to depart your Magick Circle. Extinguish the altar candles and incense. Now you are ready to go fishing, assured of success and with the blessings of the Goddess.

Comment: As much as possible do your fishing during the waxing of the New Moon.

The Huntsman's Spell

Use the same preparation as you did in the Fisherman's Spell, except fashion an image of the animal you are hunting and word the invocation to the Goddess as follows:

> *Hear ye, Gracious Goddess, I dedicate this rite to*
> *you. Bless Thou this sacred* (name of animal) *that I*
> *have fashioned and ere I send it forth into the*
> (field, woods, forest, etc.) *it shall draw the* (name
> of animal) *before my* (gun, arrows, etc.). *Rejoicing*
> *I shall return home with my kill and I shall give*
> *Thee thanks.*

Give the Ancient Gods license to depart your Magick Circle. Extinguish the candles and incense and go hunting, knowing that you will succeed at your task.

The Undines:
A Rite of Manifestation

Time: At midnight on the Midsummer night or at Full Moon Esbat.

Articles needed for the rite:

1. Athame—to inscribe the Magick Circle in the sand.

2. Incense—for a pleasing aroma before the Gods.

3. A Pentacle—a pendant, or necklace, or ring, if inscribed with the Pentagram and the sigils of the powers of the Moon will be fine.

4. If you have moonstone rings, necklaces, or pendants, wear them.

5. If you do not care to celebrate sky clad, put on something sheer. (Modern nightie sets are marvelous for this ceremony.)

The Fire: If you can, build the fire with sandalwood, cedar, and juniper. When the flame burns low, cast on a handful of incense. If you cannot obtain these three woods, use whatever driftwood you can find. If you cannot have a wood fire, then use a censer with charcoal for the fire.

When the Moon has risen to its fullest (midnight) draw your Magick Circle in the sand with your Athame. Outside your Magick Circle draw a Magick Triangle pointing toward the sea.

Within the Triangle draw the sigil of the elemental spirit of Water with red ink.

Light your fire and cast incense upon it. The Priestess (or a member of the group) holds the Pentacle in her hand. In the background soft music is played, either by tape recorder or by one of the group. (Flute or pipe music is beautiful for this rite.) Consecrate your Circle and invoke the Guardian Spirits of the North, East, South, and West to bear witness to your rite and to stand guard over the celebrants. Place censer (or fire) in the center of the Circle. The High Priestess leads the dance (slowly, dreamily) around the Circle. As you move around the Circle and the Moon shines upon your face, lift your arms high toward the Moon. The High Priestess chants an Invocation to the Old Ones and to the Moon Goddess for their aid and blessing.

High Priestess:

> *Come unto us Ancient Wise Ones. Guard our rites,*
> *ere we've begun, aid us now! We implore Thee, by*
> *standing stone and shining sea! SO MOTE IT BE!*
> *Harrahya!*

High Priestess now invokes the Moon Goddess:

> *Ea Binah, Ge!*
> *Isis unveiled, hear my plea!*
> *Shaddai, El chai Ea, Binah Ge!*
> *O soundless, boundless, bitter sea,*
> *I am Thy Priestess, Come unto me!*
> *Flower of the foam,*
> *Golden Aphrodite!*
> *Hear and appear,*
> *We know Thee near!*
> *Isis unveiled*
> *Shaddai, El Chai!*
> *Ea, Binah, Ge!*

Everyone faces toward the sea and the High Priestess invokes the undines to appear. The music continues softly. You may dance, couples or singles, or you may sit quietly.

The undines will manifest on the waves—on the surface of the sea.

To close the rite, carry the Athame and Pentacle to the four cardinal points: East, South, West, and North. All give a salute and the High Priestess gives the undines license to depart. The Guardian Spirits of the North, East, South, and West are hailed and thanked and licensed to depart. Cast more incense on the fire if you have used a censer. Carry it around the Circle, then cast the contents into the sea.

The Call of Nine

> *Gracious Goddess*
> *Holy and Divine,*
> *Answer to the Call of Nine.*
>
> *One—I stand before Thy Throne,*
> *Two—I invoke Thee alone,*
> *Three—I hold aloft my Blade,*

Four—Descend! as the Spell is made
Five—Lend Thy Power to give it Life,
Six—Thy Power! into my Knife.
Seven—On earth, in sky, and shining sea,
O Gracious Goddess, be with me.
Eight—Come now! the call is made,
Nine—Give Thy Power unto my Blade!
SO MOTE IT BE!

Gran'pa Jeff Bradley's Ritual for Stopping Bleeding

Lord
And when I pass by Thee,
And saw Thee polluted,
In Thine own blood,
I said unto Thee:
"When Thou was't
In Thy blood, LIVE!"
Yea, I said unto Thee,
"When Thou was't
In Thy blood,
LIVE!"

Lady Sheba Self-Blessing Ritual

Before performing any rite or ritual, you should always perform a self-cleansing or self-blessing ritual.

Put a few drops of your personal Holy Oil in the palm of one hand, then rub your palms together to distribute the oil evenly over the inside of your hands, saying:

Gracious Goddess,
Bless and Purify me
That I may:
See no evil (place hands over eyes);

Hear no evil (place hands over cars);
Speak no evil (place hands over mouth);
So mote it be.

Comment: This ritual belongs to my family; it was given to a Queen Witch on the astral plane. As a reminder for us, a small statue of three wise monkeys, kids, or ancient magi are carved as one statue and kept by the fireplace. This is a reminder for us to:

Never search for evil (see no evil);
Never listen to gossip (hear no evil);
Never give voice to evil (speak no evil).

The Sacred Onion Rite

I, Sheba, being on the astral plane, was instructed by the Gracious Goddess to make due sacrifice. The Goddess spoke unto me these words:

*The onion is and ever was sacred to the Gods.
In ancient times in Egypt the onion was grown in
the "Garden of the Gods," and tended by the
Priesthood. The white onion is especially holy unto
the Moon Goddess Isis. Slice a white onion
round-wise and place one white onion ring around
the wick of the candle on the altar where you say
your daily prayers. You will hear of someone dying.
When you are told of this news make the onion
sacrifice as you have been told.*

Comment: I have followed her instructions. The first sacrifice I made was most unusual. The entire candle and onion ring was consumed by flame. The flame became very high and extremely hot and filled the entire cup that held the candle. This was the only time that flames consumed the entire sacrifice. My sacrifice was accepted by the Gods.

The Adoration of Diana
A Request for Wisdom

Time: Esbat Full Moon.

Place: Outdoors under the open sky.

The High Priest casts the Magick Circle. The High Priestess invokes the Watchers of the North, East, South, and West. She purifies salt and water and purifies the Magick Circle. She blesses the cakes and wine.

The coveners enter the Magick Circle and all are purified. The High Priestess assumes the Goddess position and speaks:

> *O My Goddess, Diana, hear my song of adoration.*
> *Hear my voice when I sing Thy praises. Hear my*
> *songs as they rise heavenward, when the Full Moon,*
> *brightly shining, fills the heavens with Thy beauty.*
> *O my beautiful Moon Goddess, hear me as I stand*
> *before Thee. See me when I reach toward heaven,*
> *when my arms reach upward toward Thee. When*
> *the Full Moon shines upon me give me Thy*
> *blessings, O Diana. Teach me of Thine ancient*
> *mysteries, ancient rites of invocation that the Holy*
> *she spoke of Thy shining glory, when she told us to*
> *entreat Thee, told us when we seek for knowledge*
> *to seek and find Thee above all others. Give us*
> *wisdom O Diana: how to bind our oppressors, how*
> *to cure the sick among us. Teach me, O Diana. Give*
> *me Thy blessings, O Great Moon Goddess. Shield*
> *me from my oppressors. Receive me as your*
> *daughter, Diana. Receive me, though I am*
> *earth-bound. Grant me ancient Wiccan knowledge.*
> *When my body lies resting nightly, speak unto thy*
> *inner spirit; teach me all Thy holy mysteries. I*
> *believe Thine ancient Promise, Thy promise unto*
> *the ancient Wicca that we who seek Thy holy*

presence will receive of Thy Wisdom. Now the Full Moon shines upon me. Hear me! I stand before Thee! Grant me wisdom! O Diana! Shield me from my oppressors! Teach me Thine holy mysteries! I sing Thy praises unto the heavens. Let Thy glory shine about me. Bless us, O gracious Queen of Heaven. Descend Thou among us; descend and conquer, Gracious Goddess.

SO MOTE IT BE.

The coveners sit down inside the Circle and meditate on the descent of the Goddess upon the High Priestess. The High Priestess remains in the Goddess position. If the Goddess descends and speaks through the High Priestess, mark her words of wisdom and know thou hast been blessed. You may ask a boon of the Goddess at this time. Allow ample time for your concentrated wills to combine and become a live force that can be used by the Goddess to manifest in the Circle.

After the Goddess speaks, the High Priest pours wine into the Chalice and holds it while the High Priestess blesses it with the Athame. The High Priestess lays the Athame on the Altar and takes the Chalice from the High Priest and sips, and also accepts a cake from the paten held by the handmaiden. The High Priestess passes the Chalice to the High Priest who sips, takes a cake, and then passes the Chalice around the Circle. All coveners sip wine and take a cake. The Chalice is passed back to the High Priestess, who must drain the cup.

Sigil

I, Sheba, being on the astral plane, did receive an ancient symbol and sigil used by the ancient Javaro Indians (head-hunters) to find any lost person or thing.

Draw this sigil on paper and point it in the direction (North, South, East, or West) where the person or object is believed to be lost and they will be found.

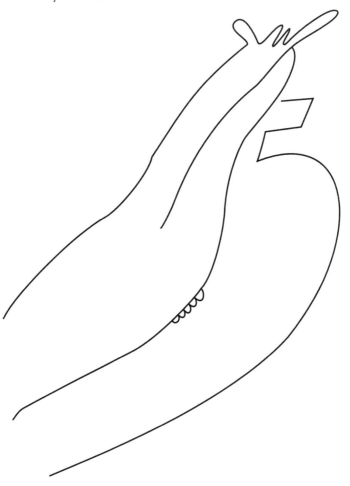

The Holy Stone Talisman

Place: A field, or park. Chant this song early, before 12 o'clock on the first day of May:

Walked I forth
On May Day Morning,
Searched I faithful,
For the round stone.
Ask I help of Great Diana,
Ask I help of Great Arida,
Found I the round stone.
Held within my hands
The golden round stone.
Lo, I cast my eyes toward Heaven,
Then tossed I the round stone
Toward the heavens; thrice
I tossed the stone toward Heaven,
Caught I the round stone,
Held I fast the round stone,
Lest the falling round stone
Return to Earth, from whence I took it.
I conjure thee, Red Goblin:
I conjure thee by Diana,
I conjure thee by Aradia,
Beautiful and Beloved Mother
Lovely Goddess of all witches,
Lovely Goddess of the Earthlings
By them did I conjure thee.
By the word of my Moon Mother,
Lovely Goddess of the moonbeams,
By them did I conjure thee.
Now I pray thee, Red Goblin,
Do not abandon, or forsake me,
For I have great need of thee.
Covered I the round stone,

With silk of red I wrapped it,
Prepared for thee a warm abode.
Rest thou inside my pocket,
Until I have need of thee.
Be thou willing to assist me,
For thou shalt do my bidding
When I call thee forth, Red Goblin.
Abidest thou within the round stone,
Until the day, when by Diana,
I release thee, to return unto the nether,
From the place whence I called thee.
SO MOTE IT BE.

Comment: Whoever carries the Holy Stone will be guarded by the spirit Red Goblin.

Look for a stone with a natural hole in it. Whenever you find it, wrap it in red silk and conjure the spirit Red Goblin and bind it to the Stone. When you have need of the Red Goblin's help, unwrap the stone and hold it in your strongest hand and mentally call the spirit forth to do your bidding.

A Beautiful Old Fire Rite to the Horned God

Before performing this rite, you should be properly prepared and purified. Cast the Magick Circle. Decorate the Altar with gifts of the season, wine and incense (pine or patchouli), water, and salt. If this rite is done out-of-doors, as it really should be, all gifts should be placed around the Cauldron. The Priestess stands in the North facing the Cauldron, holding a broom or a phallic-tipped Wand in her hand. After the Magick Circle has been sealed, the Priestess raises the staff high over the Cauldron and invokes:

Great One of the Mighty Realm of the Gods,
Who holds the Power of the Sun in Thy Hands,
I (we) invoke Thee in Thine ancient names,
Michael, Herne Bel, Balin, Lough, Arthur!
Come again! As of old into this Thy land.

Lift up Thy Shining Spear, Excalibur, to protect us.
Put to flight the Powers of Darkness,
Give us fair woodlands and green fields,
Blossoming orchards and ripening corn.
Bring us to stand upon Thy Hill of Vision,
Show us the path to the lovely Realms of the Gods.

At this point the Priestess motions the Priest to stand before her. The Priestess gives the Priest the five-fold kiss and draws the invoking Pentagram on his chest with his Wand. The Priest, who has been standing before her in the God position, accepts the Wand with a kiss. As the Priestess draws the Pentagram on the chest of the Priest, she says:

Dread Lord of Death and Resurrection,
Whose name is Mystery and Mysteries,
The Giver of Life and Lord of Life within ourselves,
Thou art Life.
Encourage Our hearts,
Let Thy Life stream in our blood,
Fulfilling our Resurrection.
For there is no part of us that is not of the Gods.
Descend, I (we) pray Thee, upon this
Thy servant and Priest.

The High Priest now plunges the Wand into the Cauldron and holds it upright, saying:

The Spear to the Cauldron,
Spirit to flesh,
Man to Woman,
Sun to Earth.

The Priest then salutes the Priestess with the Wand over the Cauldron. The Priestess takes the Aspergillus and stands by the Cauldron. Dancing around the Cauldron, the Priest and coveners now pass her. The Priestess sprinkles each one, saying:

Dance Ye about the Cauldron of Kerridwen, blessed
by Earth and Fire, Water and Wind. And be Ye
doubly blessed with the touch of this consecrated
water, even as the Sun, the Lord of Life and Light
arriveth, in his strength, in the Sign of the Waters
of Life.

Wine and cakes are passed, the Watchers dismissed and the Circle closed. The participants now feast and dance the Saraband.

Comment: This is the one rite in which the manifestation of the Great God is invoked by the last name called out.

Grandmother said that this is the rite to make Arthur manifest in the person of whomever he is in this life. I have known Arthur in two past lives. I have also known Lancelot in two past lives. Lancelot returned to me as Lafayette. I have found Arthur again and Camelot; but I have yet to find Lancelot.

If you want to invoke Pan or Dionysus, call their names last, when calling out the ancient names of the Great Horned One.

An Ancient Scottish Rite to the Horned God

HEKAS! HEKAS! ESTE BIBELOI!
HE-KAS! HEKAS! ESTE BIBELOI!
HEKAS! HEKAS! ESTE BIBELOI!
HAIL KERNUNNOS! (to the east)
HAIL KERNUNNOS! (to the south)
HAIL KERNUNNOS! (to the west)
HAIL KERNUNNOS! (to the north)
From the Almathean Horn, pour forth Thy
   Store of love.
I lowly bend before Thee, I adore Thee.
At the end, when other Gods
Are fallen and put to scorn,
I with loving Sacrifice Thy Shrine adorn.
Thy foot is to my lips, my sighs inborne.
My prayers upborne upon the rising incense smoke

Rise, touch and curl about Thy Heart.
O Great Horned One!
Spend Thine Ancient love and pity—
Descend! O Mighty One!
To aid me and bring me good luck—
Without Thee, I am lonely and forlorn.

(Pause and speak aloud your boon of the God, then say:)

FROM THE CAULDRON OF KERRIDWEN,
BLESSED BY EARTH FIRE, WATER AND WIND,
WINGED WONDER OF THE AIR,
PEGASUS! BRING TO ME MY DESIRE.
HORSE! HATTOCK, TO HORSE AND AWAY!

Comment: Please remember to use the Third Horn in this Rite. The Sacrifice spoken of in this Invocation can be your Chalice of wine, a bough of green pine, a piece of bread dipped in salt; or if the rite is being done to the Gracious Goddess, a single flower will do nicely. This rite was originally done in the open air in a woodland. It can be done of course within your home.

I caution you who do this rite to take care to obey all the preparatory Rules and Laws of the Art, for this is a very ancient and most powerful rite.

If you have a garden or a patio in which you can have some greenery, it can be the most beautiful setting for this rite. It is one of my most favored spells. It is one you can step into your garden and do every morning—a very lovely way to begin your day. Put yourself in the mood while you are taking your daily bath. Wrap yourself in a robe, or bath towel, or walk naked (careful, don't shock your neighbors) before your shrine and do this rite. It only takes a short time and when done daily keeps growing more powerful. Remember that the flower-wreathed shrine of our Goddess insures us food and shelter. I urge you who read this rite to try it for the period of one Full Moon to the next.

SO MOTE IT BE.

Ancient Rite of Drawing Down the Moon

This rite call be performed inside your home if you feel you must and if you have no way to celebrate it under the open sky. You must have a window through which you can see the Moon. Whatever happens during this rite, keep your cool, and do not be afraid. Keep calm, for this is a primitive, cosmic, and highly mystical experience.

Wrap your magick binding Cord around your waist and settle yourself comfortably underneath the open sky, under the Full Moon, at exactly the witching hour of midnight, on the first night of the Full Moon. Let the moonlight shine upon you if possible. Concentrate on drawing the Moon down around you. Use your mind power and draw the Moon down until it envelopes you. The Gracious Goddess may manifest at this point in the rite. Ask what you will and it shall be granted. If you do not see her, don't worry, she is there. When the Moon comes down around you, it is but a physical, magickal power manifestation of the Goddess. She has promised us that whatever we ask will be granted, so be very careful what you ask for.

Make sure you won't be disturbed during this ceremony because if your concentration is broken it will be twenty-eight days before you can try again. You may perform this rite alone or with a group. This may appear at first to be a very simple rite, but it is a very, very, powerful ceremony.

Rite to Receive a True Dream

Cast your Magick Circle. Set up your Altar in the North. Purify yourself, Circle, and Altar with holy water. Light candles and incense (Vision incense). Invoke the Watchers to the East, South, West, and North. Prepare a solution from myrrh, and with it write this text on a piece of white paper as follows:

KEIMI, KEIMI,
I AM THE GREAT ONE,
IN WHOSE MOUTH RESTS MOMMONA,
THOTH, NAMUMBRE, KARIKHA,

KENYRYO, PAARMINATHON,
THE SACRED IAN IEE IENACOI,
WHO IS ABOVE THE HEAVEN.
I NAMED THY GLORIOUS NAME,
THE NAME FOR ALL NEEDS.
PUT THYSELF IN CONNECTION WITH
  (your name),
HIDDEN ONE, GOD, WITH RESPECT TO
  THIS NAME,
WHICH APOLLOBEX ALSO USED.

Write also on this piece of paper the dream which you desire to receive. In ancient Egypt, a black cat was sacrificed, and the paper with the writing on it placed in the cat's mouth, and then the cat was buried. I suggest you make a black cat image of black wax and place the text in the mouth of the image, and then burn it on the coals of your Thurible. Cast on more incense when you do this. Then dismiss the Watchers and close the Circle.

From the Sacred Magic
of the Great Prophet Moses

This rite is used to heal possession by spirits or enchantments. The Magick Circle is cast and the Altar is placed in the East of the Circle. Use two white or green candles on the Altar. Light the candles and incense. (Use Moses type incense.) Purify yourself and the Circle. Face East and invoke:

> *In the name of the Lord of all the Holy Ones, may*
> *this Sword be effectual to do my services, and may*
> *the Lord of it approach to serve me and may all*
> *these powers be delivered over to me, so that I may*
> *be able to use them as they were delivered to Moses,*
> *son of Amram, perfect from his God and no harm*
> *befalling him.*

Pick up one of the altar candles and drip an outline of a man's form on virgin parchment, with arms outstretched. Under the right hand draw the image of a little man, and write on his forehead "Ariel." At his feet draw an image of another little man, in red ink, for this represents an angel appointed over fire, and write on his forehead the name "Lahabiel." Under this man write the following conjuration:

> *I conjure thee, Raphael, thou and thy servants, who*
> *are called by thy name, and whose name is*
> *included in their names RAHABIEL PHANIEL*
> *ARIEL, LAHABIEL in the name of AZBUGA, that*
> *thou healest* (name of sick or possessed person)
> *from all illness, from all hurt, and from all evil*
> *spirits. Sela Sela Sela* (Amen Amen Amen) *in the*
> *name of the most high God, Yod He Vau He. So*
> *mote it be. Depart now thou holy angels and spirits*
> *unto thine own holy abode and may there ever be*
> *peace between thee and me. Yod He Vau He,*
> *Blessed Be.*

New Moon and Candle Rite for Increase in Silver Money

"Be thou clean in mind and body." Do the Lady Sheba Self-Blessing Ritual. Anoint a tall white taper (candle) with your personal holy oil, and dedicate it to the Moon Goddess.

On the first night of the New Moon at the exact hour of midnight, light the tall white taper and carry it in your left hand.

Carry some silver coins in your right hand and go forth into the night. (Your yard will do fine.) You must be able to see the New Moon and if possible stand in the rays of the moonlight.

As you lift your face to gaze upon the Moon, say:

> *Greetings my Lady Moon,*
> *Gracious Goddess.*
> *Before all of Heaven*

And all of Earth,
I bow before Thee.

At this point bow.

Bless Thou me.
O Giver of Life
And Queen of Heaven,
See how I turn the Silver
Over and over in my hand

(Hold outstretched palm with Silver turned up toward the Moon.)

Keep now
Thine Ancient Promise,
Unto all Thy children
Who keep the turning of the Silver
For a mighty increase.

(Turn the Silver over.)

Lady Moon,
Queen of Heaven,
Granter of Abundance,
Gracious Goddess.
Binah of the Sea,
Bless Thou me.
SO MOTE IT BE!

Carry your taper back inside and extinguish the flame. Do this same ritual each night as the New Moon waxes stronger, until the midnight hour of the first night of the Full Moon. On this night allow your candle to burn completely out. The Moon will be at its zenith of power and the height of its glory at midnight on the first night of the Full Moon.

Comment: This is a very ancient ritual and I dearly love it; it is so pure and beautiful. Always chart the midnight hour by dividing the hour of sunset and sunrise. This will give you the exact hour of midnight.

Invocation to the
Great Horned God Kernunnos:
To Tie a Love Knot

For the object link you must have three red cords, or twine, or yarn spun from the male goat. (The last is best, but it is hard to obtain.) In addition to the link, secure a lock of hair, or at least several hairs (taken from the hairbrush of the intended victim).

Time: Thursday, 8:00 A.M., 3:00 P.M., 10:00 P.M.

Preparation: Arrange your Altar with special decorations pleasing to the Great Horned God Kernunnos. Use your set of ritual horns, pine cones, evergreens, oak leaves, and flowers of late autumn. Burn only the special Kernunnos incense in your Thurible. Use only red Kernunnos candles.

Cast your Magick Circle and inside the Circle draw a large equilateral Triangle, large enough to contain the Altar with room enough for you to move around. On the Altar in the center trace a large Triangle. (Both Triangles face East.) Place a red candle on each side of the Altar Triangle. Place your Chalice of wine in the center of the Altar Triangle. (Use the deepest red wine for this rite.) Bless the Chalice of wine with your Athame. If you have taped or chalked the Magick Circle and the Triangle, do not forget to retrace them with the holy Athame. Bless the water and salt in the name of Kernunnos. Purify the Circle, yourself, the Altar, and everything on it with the holy water in the name of Kernunnos.

Face East and invoke the Great Horned God Kernunnos. As you invoke, bring all the power of your witches' pyramid into action. As you invoke, anoint the sides of the Altar Triangle with wine from the Chalice, mentally dedicating the Altar to Kernunnos. Chant the ancient Kernunnos Invocation:

> *EKO EKO AZARAK,*
> *EKO EKO ZOMELEK,*
> *EKO EKO ARIDA,*
> *EKO EKO KERNUNNOS,*
> *BEZABI, LACHA, BACHABABA.*
> *LAMACH CAHI ACHABABA,*

*KARRELOS, CAHI, ACHABABA
LAMACH LAMACH BACHAROUS,
CARBAHAJI, SABALYOS,
BARYLOS.
LAZOS, ATHAME, CALYOLAS,
SAMAHAC, ET FAMYOLAS,
HARRAHYA!*

Invoke to the East, chanting the Invocation to Kernunnos. Repeat the entire invocation chanting to the South, West, and to the North, moving clockwise is you invoke. As you return to face the East the second time, KNOW that the Great Horned God is just outside your Magick Circle in the East. HE WILL MANIFEST. The Great Horned God of love, lust, and fiery passion may manifest as the Sabbatical Goat with eyes blazing and the rank smell of the he-goat pervading your Circle. The goat has been the symbol for lust and passion since time began. The God Kernunnos has a great sense of humor and will take delight in scaring you. Perhaps he will manifest as Pan or Robin Hood. If you are a female celebrating this rite and he appears as Pan or as Robin Hood, do not become enchanted and step outside your Triangle and Circle. It matters not how much courage you have, the manifestation of the tremendous, terrifying, and awesome power of the Great God Kernunnos will positively shake you. Keep your cool and as you finish the list chant, pick up the three pieces of red Cord and consecrate them with wine from the Chalice and incense (pass Cords through smoke of the incense) in the name of Kernunnos. Knot the three ends together (one end of each cord) and plait, braiding in the strand of your victim's hair is you braid the Cord. As you plait repeat the following:

*Holy Kernunnos,
I ask of Thee.
Let* (name of victim) *no pleasure,
Sleep or solace see,
Till heart and loins
Be turned to me.*

When the plaited Cord is fully twined, knot the three loose ends together firmly, binding the act and saying:

As I will!
It shall be done!
As I will
So mote it be!

If you are female you must wear this binding Cord around the upper thigh as close to your crotch as possible for twenty-eight days. If you are a male celebrant, wear the binding Cord around the genitals for twenty-eight days. Try to perform this rite on the last Thursday before the Full Moon, when the Moon is waxing strong and beautiful.

If you are not happy with the results after twenty-eight days, you perform again the Invocation to Kernunnos. Cast your Magick Circle, Triangle, and decorate the Altar as before. This time the Chalice will contain red wine, olive oil, honey, some of your urine, and three drops of your blood. Invoke the Great Horned God Kernunnos at the four cardinal points as before, and remove the Cord from your leg (or genitals). Tie nine knots in it, beginning at one end (loop a knot), then going to the other (loop another knot). Work toward the center thusly:

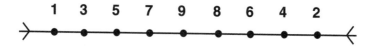

As you loop each knot, invoke Kernunnos:

Holy Kernunnos,
I ask of thee,
Let (name of victim) *no peace*
Or pleasure see,
Till heart and loin
He comes to me.

As you loop your last knot and finish the last chant, with all the power within you, literally scream, "As I will, so mote it be!"

Drop your Cord into the Chalice (so that a few drops of the wine mixture will cling to it) in the name of Kernunnos. Then cast the Cord into the fiery red coals of the burning Thurible. Cast on some of the Kernunnos incense. As you do this, bring all the fiery lust and burning passion within you into focus and say:

URE SPIRITUS IGNE,
RENES NOSTROS ET COR NOSTRUM,
FIAT, FIAT, FIAT.

Comment: To cause a breakup of a marriage or of lovers, do this spell in reverse. This is the most ancient and powerful of spells for lovers. It takes great courage and determination to perform this ancient rite for lust and passion.

Seven-Day Candle Ritual
To Fascinate and Win the One You Love

I, Sheba, using myself as all example, will teach you how to do a candle ritual to obtain the love of a man.

I am Cancer, therefore I need one silver astral candle to represent me, and I will cut or draw a Pentagram on my candle. I will also write my name on this candle.

My husband is Pisces. I need one ocean-blue astral candle to represent him, and I will write his name on his astral candle.

I will also need five red candles for power. On my candleboard I will arrange the candles as pictured in the diagram below.

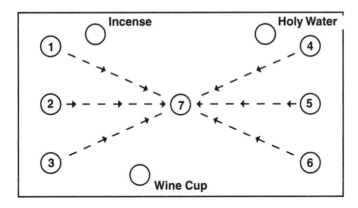

I will anoint all candles with Holy Love Oil. I will anoint my silver astral candle number two and the five red power candles with Holy Oil of High John the Conqueror. I will also anoint my candle with Lodestone Magnetic Oil. As I anoint each candle I place it on the candleboard exactly thirteen inches from the center. Candles one and four are red power candles; candles three and six are red power candies. Candle number two is my astral color candle; candle number five represents my husband; candle number seven is the offertory candle, the symbol of united love coming before the Gods. I will also pick a fresh white flower and lay it at the base of candle number seven. Now I will anoint my Altar, my candleboard, and everything on it with holy water, in the name of Arida, the Moon Goddess. Next I will light my incense, which is Moon Goddess Incense for All Lovers. Next I light candles one to six, in that order. Now I pick up candle number seven from off the board and with a new pen I write my wish upon it. As I write, I chant:

> *Gracious Goddess,*
> *Upon this Candle I will write,*
> *What I receive of thee this night.*
> *Grant what I wish you to do,*
> *I dedicate this rite to you.*
> *I trust that you will grant this boon,*
> *O Lovely Goddess of the Moon.*

I replace the candle in the center of the candleboard and light it. Then I raise my arms high and wide (representing the horns of the New Moon) and in the Goddess position I chant:

> *I call Earth to bond my Spell,*
> *Air speed its travel well,*
> *Fire give it Spirit from above,*
> *Water quench my spell with love.*
> *SO MOTE IT BE!*

I will allow all candies to burn seven minutes from the moment of lighting. Then I will extinguish all candles but number seven, which I allow to burn out completely. Then I will salute the Goddess with the Chalice and sip the wine while gazing on candle number seven. I look at it and concentrate on my husband and visualize the love union already obtained on the astral plane (remember the universal law, "As above, so below").

On the second day I will again anoint a red number-seven candle and place it in the center of the candleboard. I will also move all candles two inches toward candle seven. I will again light all candles and repeat the same invocation as on the first day. I will allow all candies to burn seven minutes, then extinguish all but number seven. I will allow this to burn completely out, while I sip the wine, concentrate, and do my visualization exercise.

I will continue to do this same ritual each day at the hour of the day in which the planetary spirit (Moon Goddess) is in strong force. Each day move the candles two inches toward center candle seven.

At the end of the ritual oil the seventh day I will allow all candles to burn completely out.

I will then cleanse my candleboard, and anything not previously consumed during the seven days will be burned by me.

Comment: It has been a witches' secret for centuries, but I'm telling you truthfully that the best time to invade the mind of another human being is the first three hours of the day, 1:00 A.M. to 3:00 A.M. But of course if you are employed and only have definite hours to work this ritual, then by all means work out your own schedule.

For all candle-burning rituals such as this one, I use a candleboard which was once a breadboard. These old breadboards can be found in antique and junk shops in every town and city. Cleansed and blessed they are ideal for candle rituals. Dripped wax is easily removed from them and they are not very likely to catch on fire during a ritual. Also a suitable piece of new board can be obtained from any lumberyard.

A Candle Ritual of Dedication
For a Specific Request

Arrange candleboard according to the diagram. Do the Lady Sheba Self-Blessing Ritual. Anoint all candles with holy oil pleasing unto the Moon Goddess. Light a Thurible of Moon Goddess incense.

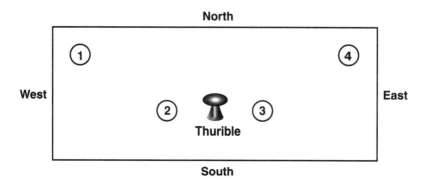

Candles one and two are white; they are anointed and dedicated to the Moon Goddess. Candle number three is a white candle of offering, anointed and dedicated to whatever purpose you seek to achieve.

Write your offering and the purpose for the ritual on a slip of paper and place it underneath candle number three.

Candle number four is your astral candle.

Light all candles. Say whatever prayer or invocation enables you to raise your vibrations. This must be your very own chant, written by you, for yourself alone. Neither I nor anyone else can tell you which chant, prayer, or invocation will heighten your vibrations and attune them to the Mother Goddess.

After the chant, sit in quiet meditation and let the candle burn.

When the offertory candle is burned halfway down, take the slip of paper from beneath candle three and burn it in the flame of the offertory candle.

When all candles are completely burned out, clean the board of wax drippings and add to the Thurible. Also add more incense at this point and allow both to burn in the Thurible.

SO MOTE IT BE!

Comment: This is an everyday, all-purpose ritual. It can be used at any hour any day, for any purpose you may desire. Anoint all candles with your personal Holy Oil.

I suggest that you use a very small candle that will only burn for one hour unless you practice yoga and can sit in meditation longer.

To Gain Control of a Man and Not Feel Guilty About It

For this ritual be properly prepared. Work in secret. Never tell another person what you are doing, since power shared is power lost. Remember that it is your own strength that makes this spell work.

Make a small fift-fath of wax or clay and wrap it in blue silk for protection from foreign vibrations of any kind.

This fift-fath represents the person you want to control. Light your candle and incense. Be single-minded in your desire. Now unwrap the fift-fath before your shrine and say:

> *Upward the Athame!*
> *Pierce the* (name of man)
> *Who hangs upside down forever*
>   (stand image on its head).
> *Astarte, Hecate, Astrothe, Dioine,*
> *Diana, Bride, Levannah,*
> *Luna, Melusine, Artemise, Aphrodite, Isis!*
> *Set me free. Set me free. Set me free.*
> *Great Mother, give me power,*
> *Let the darkness not descend,*
> *Oh, Kerridwen*
> *Give me power, keep free my mind.*
> *Set free my mind and body,*
> *Give me power, Oh Kerridwen!*

Rewrap the fift-fath. Return it to a tight place and hide it from all prying eyes.

A Spell to Tie a Man to His Bed

Dip a red thread or cord into the Cauldron. Bless the cord with fire, earth, or incense (wind), or by breathing on it. Bless the rowan cross in the same way. As you knot the cord (or thread) into a Witches' Ladder, now chant:

> *From the Cauldron of Kerridiwen*
> *Blessed by Fire, Earth, Water, and Wind*
> *Rowan tree and red thread,*
> *Tie him fast to his own bed.*

When you have finished the ladder, say:

> *Silver Moon and golden Sun,*
> *End Ye well*
> *What is here begun.*

Comment: After you have finished with the knotting, wrap the ladder around the equal-armed cross of rowan wood. When the spell is complete, wrap the corded rowan cross in a piece of red silk and put it in a tight place away from prying eyes.

Curse of the Mirrored Light

This is the most powerful rite of self-defense that I know. (And we all have the *right* to self-defense!) If you are attacked on the Inner Planes, turn the attack around, send it back, and your enemy will suffer only to the degree that he sought to harm you.

While you can always depend only on the imagination—and you can never work without the imagination—it is also well to use actual physical objects to strengthen and bring into the physical plane the energies you are utilizing. For this "curse" you can purchase six small square mirrors and glue them together in a cube with the mirrors all facing inward. Leave the top open, or hinged with cloth tape, so that you can place a picture, or any other link with the enemy in the box. When the rite is completed, seal the box up and bury it, if at all possible in a place where it will never be disturbed.

Cast your Circle with the Sword actually cutting into the ground. Use three red or black candles on the Altar, and use patchouli for incense, with a pinch each of saltpeter, sugar, and sulfur added. Drink a shot of liquor—not enough to get silly, but enough to relax your body and warm the blood. Using a soft chalk or other marker, draw a zigzag pattern on the bared chest, on the back of the robes, on the blades of the Athame and Sword, and on the ends of your Magick Cord. At the Altar, place a Staff or Sword pointing toward the source of the attack—if you know it, but otherwise pointing toward the northwest. At the four Quarters, place Staff, Broom, and Axe. Draw a Banishing Pentagram at each Quarter.

Now invoke the Goddess in her vengeful form—as Diana the Huntress, or as Melusine, and the Horned God as Thor or Saturn. Invoke the Archangels and any other entities that you are especially close to, to stand guard and help you as friends.

Most important, all the coveners will now tread the Circle, following the one who is being attacked. The victim should describe the injuries he has suffered, as well as the nature of the attack. He should build up a great emotion of indignation and self-righteous anger. If he knows the person attacking him by name, he should use that name. He should state that he wishes only to return the attack to the sender. He should use phrases and words that call for response and repetition by the coveners following him as he treads the Circle with growing anger. The coveners must also feel anger. Now describe the attacker, actually or symbolically, so that all can visualize a clear picture of the target. Place the visualized image in the imagined mirrored box (or put some object into the physical mirrored box, if you have one, at the center of the circle). Visualize the target in the box of mirrors, and see arrow-like energies being sent out from him, bouncing off the mirrors to return to him.

Continue treading the Circle, but move in toward the Center as the emotions rise to a peak, and you feel and see the Cone of Power being built. At the peak of emotion, move close to the Center, and fire the Cone at the target. Let all your emotions be directed at the target in the box, and then visualize the box being scaled up. Now let all the energies drain out of you—knowing that the rite has been successful.

Close the ritual in the usual way.

Eight-Day Candle Ritual To
Boggle the Mind of Your Enemy

Arrange your candleboard according to the diagram. Write on a piece of paper in precise words exactly what purpose is to be accomplished by this ritual. Place the paper on the candleboard so that the exact words can be said each day.

Candle zero in the center of the diagram represents your enemy. Anoint this candle with Confusion Oil and cut the enemy's name on it. If you possibly can, use a candle in your enemy's astral color.

Candles two through thirteen are black confusion candles anointed with confusion and domination oil.

Candle number one is your astral candle, with a Pentagram and your name cut on it. Anoint your astral candle with High John the Conqueror and Domination Holy Oil.

Candles ⊗ ⊗ are red power candles with pentagrams cut on them They are anointed with protection oil. Their energy vibrations protect and strengthen the vibrations of your astral candle.

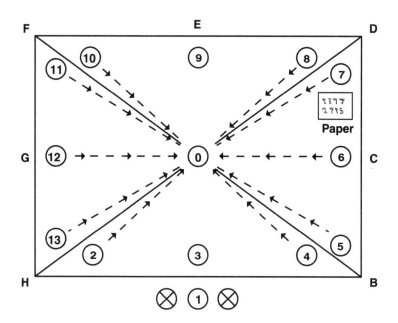

First Day: Light candle number one and the red power candles first at position A.

Next, light candles two through thirteen.

Then light candle zero in the center of the diagram.

Chant your command (that which is on the paper on the candleboard) you light the candles. Continue chanting your command as long is the candles burn. Let all candles burn eight minutes, then extinguish the flames.

Extinguish the enemy candle zero first. Next extinguish candles thirteen through two. Next extinguish the two red power candles. Last of all, extinguish your astral candle number one.

Second Day: Do the entire ritual as on the first day. Move the two red power candles and your astral candle from position A to position B. Also, start the stalking of your enemy by moving the black confusion candles two inches toward the center enemy candle.

Third Day: Do the entire ritual as on the first day. Move the two red power candles and your astral candle from position B to position C. Move the black confusion candles two inches nearer the center candle.

Fourth Day: Do the entire ritual as on the first day. Move the two red power candles and your astral candle to position D. Move all black candles two inches toward the center candle.

Fifth Day: Do the entire ritual as on the first day, moving the two red power candles and your astral candle to position E. Move the black candles two inches closer to the center candle.

Sixth Day: Do the entire ritual as on the first day. Move the two red power candles and your astral candle to position F. Move the black candles two inches closer to the center candle.

Seventh Day: Do the entire ritual as on the first day and move the two red candles and your astral candle to position G. Move the black candles two inches nearer the center candle.

Eighth Day: Do the entire ritual as on the first day. Move the two red power candles and the astral candle to position H. Move the black candles to form a tight circle enclosing the center candle.

Before the black candles, red candles, and your astral candle burn out move your red candles and your astral candle from position H to position A. Thus you have encircled the enemy in all four quarters of the universe, East, North, West, and South. Let all candles burn completely out.

Always select a shorter candle for the enemy or adversary, so it will be absolutely sure to burn out before any of the other candles.

As always, whenever a ritual is completed and the flames have gone out, scrape the candle drippings from your candleboard and burn in fire or bury in the earth. I much prefer to burn the remains of my rituals.

Comment: This is a very, very, powerful ritual; give it much thought before commencing. Keep your mind in complete command throughout the entire ritual. Be sure the need to use this ritual is just and that the enemy deserves its effects.

A Candle Ritual to Overcome a Psychic Attack or Crossed Condition

First Day: Take a salt water bath into which a teaspoon of King Solomon Success Holy Oil has been added.

Do the Lady Sheba Self-Blessing Ritual to invoke the help of the Gracious Goddess. Light incense pleasing to the Moon Goddess. Arrange candleboard according to the diagram.

Write your invocation on clean paper and place on the candleboard.

⊙, your astral candle, is anointed with High John the Conqueror Oil or Solomon Success Oil. Cut a pentagram and your name on this candle. (Use your Bolline for cutting.)

⊗, a blue protection candle, is anointed with Holy Protection Oil.

The center candle, number five, is the source of psychic attack or crossed vibrations. Anoint this candle with Confusion Oil and sprinkle a small amount of graveyard dust over the candle.

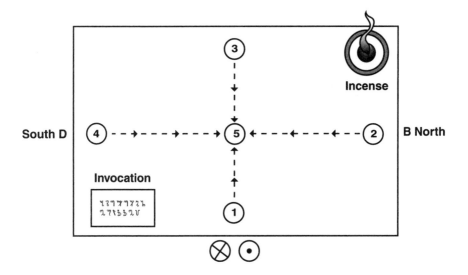

Candles one through four are white candles anointed with holy domination oil.

Light the blue protection candle and your astral candle. Then light candles one through four. Light the center candle last. Let all candles burn twenty-eight minutes. While they burn chant this invocation:

> *Gracious Goddess, Hear me! I entreat Thee,*
> *For I feel the dark swift arrows,*
> *Of some unknown, unenlightened enemy.*
> *Thou who knowest the hearts of men,*
> *Shield me, I implore Thee.*
> *Thou Who see'st all, Thou Who knowest all,*
> *Break! the arrows in their flight.*
> *Return! them unto their Sender!*
> *Gracious Goddess,*
> *Bless me, bless me, bless me.*
> *Gracious Goddess,*
> *Purify fire, purify me purify me.*
> *Gracious Goddess,*
> *So mote it be. So mote it be.*
> *So mote it be!*

Extinguish the candles, starting first with five, then four through one, then the blue protection candle and the astral candle.

Second Day: Take the same bath as on the first day and do the Lady Sheba Self-Blessing Ritual.

Repeat the entire ritual of the first day, except move the blue protection candle and your astral candle from the East quarter of position A to the North quarter or B position. This is traveling widdershin (symbolically) around the four quarters of the universe. Also move candles one through four, to a position two inches closer to the center candle.

Third Day: Take the salt water bath as on the first day and do the Lady Sheba Self-Blessing Ritual. Repeat the entire ritual as on the first day, moving the blue protection and astral candles from the North quarter or B Position to the West quarter or C position. Move candles one through four, to a position two inches closer to the center candle.

Fourth Day: Take the salt water bath and do the Self-Blessing Ritual. Repeat the entire ritual as on the first day, moving the blue protection and astral candle to the South quarter or D position. Move candles one through four, to a position two inches closer to center candle number five.

Fifth Day: Take the salt water bath and do the Purification Ritual.

Repeat the entire ritual is on the first day, moving the blue protection and astral candles from the South quarter or D position to the East quarter or A position. Move candles one through four into the center and surround the center candle. Let all candles burn completely out.

Cleanse your candleboard of any candle drippings and burn all remains from the ritual in a fireplace, Thurible, Cauldron, or wherever you can have an open flame.

Now light incense and a small white candle that has been anointed with your personal Holy Oil. Relax and visualize the Gracious Moon Goddess. Thank Her for dispelling your crossed condition or psychic attack.

6

The Recipes

Kernunnos Incense

Patchouli leaves (powdered)
Bay leaves (powdered)
Pine needles (powdered)
Wormwood stems and leaves (powdered)
Vervain leaves (powdered)

Mix and moisten with a few drops of:

Deep red wine
Olive oil
Pine oil
Clove oil
Honey
3 drops of your own blood
3 drops of your urine
A clash of red pepper
A clash of ginger

Prepare this incense on a Thursday when the New Moon is waxing strong.

Kernunnos Perfume

Use equal amounts of:

> Patchouli oil
> Cedarwood oil
> Pine oil

Add the following items:

> 3 drops geranium oil
> 3 drops rose essence
> 3 drops jasmine essence
> 3 drops ilang-ilang essence
> 3 drops vanilla
> 3 drops clove oil

Note: You can use patchouli oil by itself, as it is holy to Kernunnos as perfume.

Moon Goddess Incense
(for All Lovers)

Use equal amounts of each:

> Storax
> White poppy
> Aloe
> Benzoe
> Rose blossoms
> Cinnamon
> Coriander seed
> Thyme
> White lily blossoms
> Pinch of pulverized camphor

Mix together and pulverize.

Moon Goddess Incense
(for a Special Request)

Use equal amounts of each:

Aloe (powdered)
White poppy seed
Storax
Benzoe
Pumpkin seed
Nasturtium seed
A few drops of wintergreen oil
Lettuce seed
White rose petals
Violet flowers
Cucumber seed
Moonwort flowers *(Osmunda lunaria)*
Cabbage seed

The Famous Abtina Incense

These four ingredients symbolize the four elements. Mix equal parts of the following:

Modern Name	Ancient Name	Element
Gum resin that resembles the herb asafetida in quality	Galbanum	Air
Gum resin of pine	Frankincense	Fire
Myrrh	Stacte	Water
Part of a shell fish or gills of a fish	Onycha	Earth

Cleopatra Incense

Mix equal amounts of the following:

>Sandalwood (powdered)
>Orris root (powdered)
>Patchouli (powdered)
>Myrrh (powdered)
>Frankincense (powdered)
>A pinch of salt
>A dash of safflower powder
>A few drops of patchouli oil to make
>   the incense stay together

Consecration Incense

Mix equal parts (powdered) of the following:

> Sandalwood
> Myrrh
> Cinnamon
> Frankincense
> Patchouli leaves
> Orris root
> Winters bark

Mix all together and add a couple of pinches of saltpeter.

Egyptian Vision Incense

Mix equal parts of the following:

> Sandalwood
> Myrrh
> Cinnamon
> Orris root (two pinches)
> Salt (a pinch)
> Olibanum
> Red food coloring

Moses Type Incense

Use equal parts of the following:

Frankincense
Myrrh

Mix with a few drops of olive oil and place on burning charcoal, or it may be mixed with a bambawood base or sandalwood base.

Teas and Ointments

The following teas and ointments come from my Gran'ma Nancy Wicker's recipes.

Balm of Gilead Bud Ointment

Gather the green buds from a Balm of Gilead tree and put them in a cauldron with sheep or beef fat. Fry slowly until the buds are small and brown (used up) and then strain into a clean jar and seal This is used as an ointment for chapped hands, dry skin, wounds, burns, and to promote growth of hair.

Personal Holy Oil

I use virgin olive oil, my own favorite perfume, and 3 drops of my blood.

I use the Blessing Ritual from *The Book of Shadows* to purify and make holy this oil, perfume, and blood mixture. Keep this tightly bottled.

I use this oil constantly. I also use this oil as a base and then in special ceremonies add another oil like High John the Conqueror or a Domination Oil. Once you realize your best perfume and start using your own Holy Oil you will find it will become your most used oil.

Comment: For Heaven's sake, use your nose to pick the scents you are attuned to. Eventually you will find a scent chemically attuned to you and it will become your all-time favorite.

Holy Love Oil

You will need:

> Olive oil
> Orrisroot (known as loveroot)

Place orrisroot in the olive oil and heat slowly to a moderate heat. DO NOT BOIL. Rebottle the oil, placing the orrisroot in the bottle also. Bless it by the ritual.

Lodestone Magnetic Oil

Combine olive oil (which contains a lodestone or magnetic sand) and your own personal exotic perfume that has been blessed by ritual.

High John the Conqueror Oil

You will need:

>Olive oil
>High John the Conqueror root

Place root in the olive oil and heat to moderate heat. Bless and rebottle it. (Leave the root in the bottled oil.)

Catnip Tea

Catnip is a wild herb. Put a few leaves in a pint of boiling water. Let it steep until the water has the catnip flavor, sweeten, and drink. This is a good sedative for your nerves and makes men amorous. Also good for winter colds and can be given to babies.

Strawberry Tea

Wild strawberry leaf tea is the greatest known source of Vitamin C.

Rue Herb Tea

Makes a tea, a stimulant, and also a nervine. Do not drink rue tea if you are pregnant; it can cause abortion.

For Sore Stiff Muscles

Take equal amounts of the following:

>Mullien leaves
>Sage leaves
>Marjoram leaves
>Chamomile flowers

Boil together and let steep. Keep sealed until needed. Massage sore muscles for relief.

King's Ointment for Your Skin

Use the herb frostwort (*helianthernun*), saffron, date wine, along with lion fat (have your husband or boyfriend get you some). In the absence of lion fat I suggest you use beef tallow. Melt items together and boil slowly for a short time. Strain and place in a jar for external use.

Tansy Leaf Tea

Steep the leaves in boiling water. Strain. Bathe your skin bruises. This will take off freckles; good for sunburn.

Eucalyptus Oil

Buy this at a drug store (it is not a native of America). Put a few drops in a vaporizer to stop coughs and to make breathing easier.

Burdock Tea

Use any part of entire plant. This herb is known worldwide as a blood purifier. The tea will ease the hurt and heal the sore, or make a poultice of burdock leaves and white of an egg for a burn.

Coltsfoot Cough Syrup

Use the leaves and flower of the wild herb. Steep in boiling water. Sweeten with honey. Good for colds. Gran'ma also smoked the dried leaves in her pipe for coughs.

Licorice Cough Syrup

Take root of plant and raisins and boil together. Then strain and add brown sugar. Boil to a syrup. Good for a choking cough.

Marigold Tea (Calendula Officinalis)

Use petals of the dried flowers. Make tea for chronic ulcers or use as a poultice for varicose veins.

This tea is also a good stimulant. Keep it around to add to broths and soups.

Slippery Elm

The inner bark, powdered, may be mixed with sugar and boiling water and eaten for stomach trouble. it may be given to babies with bowel problems. It is good for bronchitis. The powdered inner bark makes one of the finest poultices for wounds of all kinds, burns, or infection of the skin.

Chamomile Flower Tea

Make a tea from the flowers; sweeten with honey. May be given to teething babies. A good sedative for adults. Drink chamomile tea regularly and always have a beautiful complexion.

Self-Heal Herb

Make a syrup of herb and water. Add sugar to taste. Take inwardly when you have a wound inside. Bruise the leaves into a poultice and apply to wounds outside the body. An ointment may be made from this herb.

For Sore Mouths or Throats

Boil together in wine and water: plantain, sage, and rosemary. Strain and add a little alum and honey. It is good for mouth rinse or as a gargle for sore throats.

The Dandelion, a Versatile Herb

The green leaves may be eaten raw as a salad, or boiled as greens, or dried and made into tea. The dried and powdered root can also be made into tea. (Use plenty of it.) Good for the kidneys and liver trouble, and it is rich in food value.

Violet Tea

Both leaves and flowers are good to use. Pour a pint of boiling water over a pint of leaves and let it steep for twelve hours. Strain. Can be cut for tea, or used as a poultice for sores. I also use green violet leaves and flowers in my summer salads.

Witch Hazel Tonic

The bark and leaves are good taken internally for stopping bleeding wounds. The leaves are a cure for pyorrhea. To make an ointment use nine parts beef tallow and one part fluid bark extract. It is also good for bleeding piles, and is a good astringent or sedative tonic.

Primrose

Use the wild flower only, and then only the root, as a tea to help rheumatism, gout, paralysis. Leaves can be made into a salve for wounds. You may take the tea one tablespoon at a time.

Myrrh

Use the oleo gum resin as a healing antiseptic and mouth wash. It is very strong. Be careful, as a few grains in a glass of water are enough.

Rosemary Rinse

Boil rosemary and water just like you make tea. Cool, then rinse your hair with it after washing to make it shine.

Vervain Herb

Make into a tea for jaundice. Will liven up your guests if you put a spot in their tea.

Ground Ivy, Alehoof

Make a tea for enjoyment. One of the best teas I know of. Can also be used for a poultice.

Golden Seal, Wild Yellow Root

This can be obtained at most drug stores. One tablespoon to one pint of boiling water makes a very bitter tonic and blood purifier. For spring and fall use.

Comment: Gran'pa took his tonic the easy way. He mixed it with a quart of moonshine whiskey. It could be mixed in almost any kind of beverage to deaden the bitter taste.

Witches' Flying Ointment

Ancient method:

3	grains annamthol
30	grains betel
50	grains extract of opium
6	grains cingfoil
15	grains henbane
15	grains belladonna
15	grams hemlock
250	grains *Cannabis indica*
5	grains canthreindin

Mix with oil of your choice.

Modern method (very amusing!):

1	jar hand cream
1	tsp. vegetable fat
2	tsp. belladonna
3	drops liquid detergent
½	tsp. wolfbane juice

Mix well and add perfume of your choice.
Aha! It seems as if we are not quite as tough as the old ones, eh?

Comment: Most of these ingredients are psychedelic and produce hallucinations. They are poisonous and illegal. I have not used these, so beware.

Sun Tan Oil

Use equal amounts of:

> Peanut oil
> Palm oil
> Sesame oil
> Safflower oil

Sun Tan Oil

Use Johnson's Baby Oil with a few drops (enough to color lightly) of tincture of iodine. Mix well, apply with love, and let the sun shine (courtesy of Nadine Wicker).

Comment: If you don't believe me, take a long took at the legs of the beautiful girls at Morehead University, Morehead, Kentucky.

Witch Hazel Cream

Use equal amounts of these two:

> Lanolin
> Petrolatum [petroleum jelly]

Melt the lanolin and petrolatum together. Heat to about 60°F. Add enough witch hazel to make a smooth cream. Add your favorite perfume.

7

The Dances

After the time of persecution by the Catholic Church and the Salem burnings, the witches' rounds were called square dancing, square being the exact opposite of round in the mind of the Church.

The witches' rounds eventually evolved into the Saturday night barn dances of early America, Many of the old rounds are still danced today under the disguise of square dancing.

As a girl growing up in the hills of eastern Kentucky, my cousins and friends and I danced these old rounds every Saturday night, the Circle Eight and the Grapevine Twist being the most beloved of all. Sometimes the dances got pretty wild and nearly always lasted from dusk until dawn.

The Circle Eight

All coveners hold hands, alternately, male-female (there are usually eight people). Someone calls the movement of the dance to fast-moving background music.

All hands up and circle left. (Coveners hold clasped hands high and dance to left, forming a complete circle.)

All the way round in a single line, ladies fore and gents behind. (Coveners unclasp hands and form a single dance line.)

Couple up four. (Two males and two females join hands, still dancing in a circle.)

Swing your opposite, then your own, grab your pardner and promenade home.

First couple out. (One couple steps into center of the circle.)

First to the right, then to the left, don't forget that two-hand swing. (Couple clasps right hands and dances round, then clasps left hands and pivots around. Then clasping two right hands and two left hands, dances around.)

Round the first lady. Lady round the lady and the gent go slow. Lady round the gent and the gent don't go. (The couple in the center dances round the first couple to the right of the space they left in the circle.)

Couple up four. First to the right and then to the left, don't forget that two-hand swing. Swing your opposite, then your own, grab your pardner and promenade home. (The couples that remain in the circle join in at the call of *Swing your opposite, then your own,* and then return to the same place, forming the original circle.)

Round the next lady. (Second lady in circle line. The center couple of dancers goes to the next couple in line and dances through the same routine and to the same call, beginning at *Round the first lady.* This continues until they have danced around and with each couple in the entire ring. When they have danced, they return to the place where they left the circle at *First couple out.* Then the next couple in line goes to the center of the circle.)

Next couple lead out. (Begin at *First to the right,* and continue to the end.)

When all couples have danced the complete circle, then the round is ended.

The Grapevine Twist

Caller:

Couple up eight and all get straight.
All lead out in a single line,
Ladies before and gents behind.
Opposite swing and then your own,
Promenade your pardner and stand alone.
First couple lead out (to center of circle).
First to the right, then to the left.
Don't forget that two-hand swing.
Grapevine twist and round the first lady
(first lady to right of space in circle).
The gent falls through the old side door,
Side couples swing and round up four,
Four in the ring, single line,
Ladies before and gents behind
Opposite swing and then your own,
Promenade your pardner and stand alone.
Grapevine twist and round next lady,
The gent falls through the old side door.
Side couples swing and round up more.
Couple up six and all get fixed.
All lead out in a single line,
Ladies before and gents behind.
Opposite swing and then your own.
Promenade your pardner and stand alone.
Grapevine twist and round the next lady.
The gent falls through the old side door.
Side couples swing and round up more.
Couple up eight and all get straight.
All lead out in a single line,
Ladies before and gents behind.
Opposites swing and then your own.
Promenade your pardner and all come home.

The dance is finished when each couple has led the entire Grapevine Twist around the circle. While the Grapevine Twist was originally danced by four couples, we always made the circle big enough to include all those who wished to dance.

(courtesy of Clyde E. Wicker, Mousie, Kentucky)

Ancient Winking or Kissing Game

Male and female sit alternately in circle, not touching each other. One man does not have a partner and has to try to get a lady from one of the other men. He chooses a lady, then winks at her. She must try to escape from her partner, who tries to catch and hold her. If she succeeds in getting to the winking man, she rewards him with a kiss for choosing her. The gentleman left without a lady now becomes the man seeking a partner by the sly wink.

After awhile the game may be reversed and the ladies wink at the men. One woman drops out to start the game, usually the High Priestess. This is a good game to play before a rite, or after when feasting and merriment are in full swing.

The Ancient Meeting Dance

Chant the ancient Kernunnos Invocation:

EKO EKO AZAREK
EKO EKO ZOMELEK
EKO EKO ARIDA
EKO, EKO KERNUNNOS
BEZABI, LACHA, BACHABABA.
LAMACII, CAHI, ACHABABA,
KARRELOS, CAHI, ACHABABA,
LAMACH, LAMACH, BACHAROUS,
CARBAHAJI, SABALYOS,
BARYLOS.
LAZOS, ATHAME, CALYOLAS,
SAMAHAC, FAMYOLAS,
HARRAHYA!

The dance is led by the High Priestess or the High Priest. The dance line is formed by males and females alternately, each clasping the waist of the person in front of them in the line. The High Priest or Messenger beats out the rhythm and speed with the Stang. The leader dances a decreasing circle from the rim of the Magick Circle to its Center. Then from the Center, the Dance unwinds again to the outer Rim. The High Priestess embraces and kisses every male as he comes opposite to Her in the Chain. Every female embraces and kisses each male as he comes opposite to her as the Dance unwinds.

> *THE GODS HAVE BEEN WORSHIPPED,*
> *THE GAMES HAVE BEGUN,*
> *THE DANCES ARE DANCED,*
> *THE OLD SONGS SUNG.*
> *KEEPERS OF THE WISDOM,*
> *STAY CLOSE TO YOUR HEARTH;*
> *FOR "MERRY WE MEET"*
> *AND "MERRY WE PART."*
> *SO MOTE IT BE*
> *BLESSED BE*

Queen Sheba
Coven of Camelot

The Book of Shadows

A Note on the Text

This book is the remnant of the ancient Religion as we have it today, fiercely guarded by Witches who saved it during the period of persecution.

The book contains all the yearly ceremonies plus other ancient rites like "Drawing Down the Moon," an exceedingly ancient and most powerful ceremony.

Most modern Witches believe that this is the right time to reveal the Book of Shadows, despite the legend concerning the "curse of the Goddess" on whoever gives this book to the world.

Note that the Book of Shadows is presented in traditional fashion, with blank pages facing each page of text. Readers may use this space for personal notations as they work with the rituals and ceremonies.

1

The Laws

Your High Priestess

In the Magic Circle, the words, commands, and every wish of the High Priestess are law.

She is the earthly, living representative of our Gracious Goddess. She must be obeyed and respected in all things. She is Our Lady and above all others, a queen in the highest sense of the word.

All female coveners must curtsy whenever they come before Her and say, "Blessed Be."

All male coveners must bend the knee and give her a kiss on the right cheek and say, "Blessed Be."

Your High Priest

He is the earthly, living representative of the Great Horned God and, in the Magic Circle, He commandeth the respect due to one who is a Magus, a Lord Counselor, and father.

The Laws

1. The Law was made and ardane of old.

2. The Law was made for the Wicca to advise and help in their troubles.

3. The Wicca should give due worship to the Gods and obey Their will, which They ardane, for it was made for the good

of the Wicca, as the worship of the Wicca is good for the
Gods. For the Gods love the brethren of the Wicca.

4. As a man loveth a woman by mastering her,

5. So the Wicca should love the Gods by mastering them.

6. And it is necessary that the 𝜙 (Magic Circle), which is the
Temple of the Gods, should be duly cast and purified that it
may be a fit place for the Gods to enter.

7. And the Wicca should be properly prepared and purified to
enter into the presence of the Gods.

8. With love and worship in their hearts, they shall raise power
from their bodies to give power to the Gods.

9. As has been taught of old.

10. For in this way only may man have a communion with
the Gods, for the Gods cannot help men without the help
of man.

11. And the High Priestess shall rule Her Coven as the
representative of the Goddess.

12. And the High Priest shall support Her as the representative
of the God.

13. And the High Priestess shall choose whom She will, if he
have sufficient rank, to be Her High Priest.

14. For, as the God himself kissed Her feet in the Fivefold salute,
laying His power at the feet of the Goddess, because of Her
youth and beauty, Her sweetness and kindness, Her wisdom
and Her justice, Her humility and gentleness and generosity,

15. So He resigned all His power to Her.

16. But the High Priestess should ever mind that all power
comes from Him.

17. It is only lent, to be used wisely and justly.

18. And the greatest virtue of a High Priestess be that She recognizes that youth is necessary to the representative of the Goddess.

19. So will She gracefully retire in favor of a younger woman, should the Coven so decide in council.

20. For the true High Priestess realizes that gracefully surrendering the pride of place is one of the greatest virtues.

21. And that thereby will She return to that pride of place in another life, with greater power and beauty.

22. In the old days, when Witches extended far, we were free and worshipped in all the greatest temples.

23. But, in these unhappy times, we must celebrate our Sacred Mysteries in secret.

24. So be it ardane, that none but the Wicca may see our mysteries, for our enemies are many and torture loosens the tongue of men.

25. So be it ardane, that no Coven shall know where the next Coven bide.

26. Or who its members be, save only the Priest and Priestess and the Messenger.

27. And there shall be no communication between them, save only by the Messenger of the Gods, or the Summoner.

28. And only if it be safe may the Covens meet in some safe place for the Great Festivals.

29. And while there, none shall say whence they come, nor give their true names.

30. To this end, that if any be tortured, in their agony, they may not tell if they do not know.

31. So be it ardane, that no one shall tell anyone, not of the Craft, who be of the Wicca, or give any names, or where any abide, or in any way tell anything which can betray any of us to our faces.

32. Nor may he tell where the Covendom be.

33. Or the Covenstead.

34. Or where the meetings be.

35. And if any break these Laws, even under torture, the Curse of the Goddess shall be upon them, so they may never be reborn on earth, and may they remain where they belong, in the Hell of the Christians.

36. Let each High Priestess govern Her Coven with justice and love, with the help and advice of the High Priest and the Elders, always heeding the advice of the Messenger of the Gods if He comes.

37. She will heed all complaints of all Brothers and strive to settle all differences among them.

38. But it must be recognized that there will always be people who will ever strive to force others to do as they will.

39. These are not necessarily evil.

40. And they oft have good ideas, and such ideas should be talked over in council.

41. But, if they will not agree with their Brothers or if they say:

42. "I will not work under this High Priestess."

43. It hath ever been the Old Law, to be convenient for the Brethren, and to avoid disputes.

44. Any of the third may claim to found a new Coven, because they live over a league from the Covenstead or are about to do so.

45. Anyone living within the Covendom and wishing to form a new Coven shall tell the Elders of their intentions and on the instant avoid their dwelling and remove to a new Covendom.

46. Members of the old Coven may join the new one when it is formed, but if they do they must utterly avoid the old Coven.

47. The Elders of the old and new Covens should meet in peace and brotherly love to decide the new boundaries.

48. Those of the Craft who live outside both Covens may join either indifferent, but not both.

49. Though all may, if the Elders agree, meet for the Great Festivals, if it be truly in peace and brotherly love.

50. But splitting the Coven oft means strife, so for this reason these Laws were made of old, and may the Curse of the Goddess be on any who disregard them!

SO BE IT ARDANE.

51. If you would keep a book (your Black Book) let it be in your own hand of write; let Brothers and Sisters copy what they will, but never let the book out of your hands and never keep the writings of another.

52. For if it be in their hand of write, they may be taken and engained.

53. Let each guard his own writings, and destroy them whenever danger threatens.

54. Learn as much as you may by heart, and when danger is past, rewrite your book an it be safe.

55. For this reason, if any die, destroy their book, an they have not been able to.

56. For, an it be found, 'tis clear proof against them.

57. And our oppressors know well: "Ye may not be a Witch alone."

58. So all their kin and friends be in danger of torture.

59. So destroy everything not necessary.

60. If your book be found on you, 'tis clear proof against you alone. You may be engained.

61. Keep all thoughts of the Craft from your mind.

62. If the torture be too great to bear, say: "I will confess. I cannot bear this torture. What do you want me to say?"

63. If they try to make you talk of the Brotherhood, do not.

64. But if they try to make you speak of impossibilities such as flying through the air, consorting with the Christian Devil, or sacrificing children or eating men's flesh,

65. To obtain relief from the torture, say, "I hold an evil dream, I was beside myself, I was crazed."

66. Not all the magistrates are bad; if there be any excuse, they may show mercy.

67. If you have confessed ought, deny it afterwards. Say you babbled under the torture, say you do not know what you said.

68. If you are condemned, fear not.

69. Fear not, the Brotherhood is powerful, they will help you to escape if you stand steadfast.

70. But if you betray ought, there is no hope for you in this life or that to come.

71. Be sure, if steadfast you go to the pyre, drugs will reach you, you will feel naught. You but go to death and what lies beyond.

The Ecstasy of the Goddess

72. To avoid discovery, let the working tools be as ordinary things that any may have in their houses.

73. Let the Pentacles be of wax so that they may be broken at once or melted.

74. Have no sword, unless your rank allows you one.

75. Have no names or signs on anything.

76. Write the names or signs on them in ink immediately before consecrating them, and wash it off immediately afterwards.

77. Do not engrave them lest they cause discovery.

78. Let the color of the hilts tell which is which.

79. Ever remember, ye are the "Hidden Children of the Goddess," so never do anything to disgrace them or her.

80. Never boast, never threaten, never say you would wish ill of anyone.

81. If any person, not in the magic circle, speak of the Craft say, "Speak not to me of such, it frightens me. 'Tis evil luck to speak of it."

82. For this reason: the Christians have their spies everywhere. These speak as if they were well affected to us, as if they would come to our meetings, saying, "My mother used to go to worship the Old Ones. I would I could go myself."

83. To such as these, ever deny all knowledge.

84. But to others, ever say: "'Tis foolish talk of Witches flying through the air. To do so they must be light as thistledown. And men say that Witches all be so bleared-eyed, old crones, so what pleasure can there be at a Witch meeting such as folks talk on?"

85. And say, "Many wise men now say there be no such creatures."

86. Ever make it a jest and in some future time, perhaps, the persecution may die and we may worship our Gods in safety again.

87. Let us all pray for that happy day.

88. May the blessings of the Goddess and God be on all those who keep these Laws which are ardane.

89. If the Craft have any Appenage, let all guard it, and help to keep it clear and good for the Craft.

90. And let all justly guard all monies of the Craft.

91. But if any brother truly wrought it, 'tis right they have their pay, and it be just. And this be not taking money for the Art, but for good and honest work.

92. And ever the Christians say, "The laborer is worthy of his hire," but if any brother work willingly for the good of the Craft without pay, 'tis to their greatest honor.

SO BE IT ARDANE.

93. If there be any quarrels or disputes among the brethren, the High Priestess shall straightly convene the Elders and inquire into the matter and they shall hear both sides, first alone, then together.

94. And they shall decide justly, not favoring the one side or the other.

95. Ever recognizing there be people who can never agree to work under others.

96. But at the same time, there be some people who cannot rule justly.

97. To those who ever must be chief, there is one answer.

98. Void the Coven, or seek another one or make a Coven of your own, taking with you those who will go.

99. To those who cannot rule justly the answer be, "Those who cannot bear your rule will leave you."

100. For none may come to meetings with those with whom they are at variance.

101. So, an either cannot agree, "Get hence, for the Craft must ever survive."

SO BE IT ARDANE.

102. In the olden days, when we had power, we could use the Art against any who ill-treated the Brotherhood. But in these evil days, we must not do so! For our enemies have devised a burning pit of everlasting fire, into which they say their God casteth all the people who worship Him, except it be the very few who are released by their priest's spells and masses. And this be chiefly by giving monies and rich gifts to receive His favor, for their God is ever in need of money.

103. But as our Gods need our aid to make fertility for man and crops, so it is the God of the Christians ever is in need of man's help to search out and destroy us. Their priests ever tell them that any who get our help are damned to this Hell forever, so men be mad with the terror of it.

104. But they make men believe that they may escape this Hell if they give Witches to the tormentors. So for this reason, all be forever spying, thinking, "An I catch but one of the Wicca, I will escape this fiery pit."

105. So for this reason we have our hidels, and men searching long and not finding say: "There be none, or if there be, they be in a far country."

106. But when one of our oppressors dies, or even be sick, ever is the cry, "This be Witches' malice," and the hunt is up again, and though they slay ten of their own to one of ours, still they care not. They have countless thousands.

107. While we are few indeed.

SO BE IT ARDANE.

108. That none shall use the Art in any way to do ill to any.

109. However much they injure us, HARM NONE and now times many believe we exist not.

SO BE IT ARDANE.

110. That this Law shall ever continue to help us in our plight. No one, however great an injury or injustice they receive, may use the Art in any way to do ill or harm any. But they may,

after great consultations with all, use the Art to restrain Christians from harming us or tax others, but only to let or constrain them.

111. To this end, men will say: "Such an one is a mighty searcher out and a persecutor of old women whom they deemeth to be Witches, and none hath done him skith, so they be proof they cannot, or more truly where be none."

112. For all know full well, that so many folk have died because someone had a grudge against them, or were persecuted because they had money or goods to seize, or because they had none to bribe the searchers. And many have died because they were scolding old women. So much that men now say that "only old women are Witches."

113. And this be to our advantage, and turns suspicions away from us.

114. In England and Scotland, 'tis now many a year since a Witch hath died the death. But misuse of the power might raise the persecution again.

115. So never break this Law, however much you are tempted, and never consent to it being broken in the least.

116. If you know it is being broken, you must work strongly against it.

117. And any High Priestess who consents to its breach must immediately be deposed. "For 'tis the blood of the Brethren they endanger."

118. Do good, and it be safe and only if it be safe.

119. And strictly keep to the old Law.

120. Never accept money for the use of the Art. For money ever smeareth the taker. "'Tis sorcerers and conjurers and priests of the Christians who ever accept money for the use of their Arts. And they sell dwale, and evil loves spells and pardons, so let men escape from their sins."

121. Be not as these. If you accept no money, you will be free from temptation to use the Art for evil causes.

122. All may use the Art for their own advantage, or for the advantage of the Craft, only if you are sure you harm none.

123. But ever let the Coven debate this at length. Only if all be satisfied and none be harmed may the Art be used.

124. If it is not possible to achieve your ends one way, perchance the aim may be achieved by acting in a different way, so as to harm none. May the Curse of the Goddess be on any who breaketh this Law.

SO BE IT ARDANE.

125. 'Tis judged lawful an any of the Craft need a house or land and none will sell, to incline the owner's mind so as to be willing to sell, providing it harmeth it not in any way and the full price is paid, without haggling,

126. Never bargain or cheapen anything whilst you live by the Art.

SO BE IT ARDANE.

127. 'Tis the old Law and the most important of all Laws that no one may do anything which will endanger any of the Craft, or bring them into contact with the law of the land, or any of our persecutors.

128. In any disputes between the brethren, no one may invoke any Laws but those of the Craft.

129. Or any tribunal but that of the Priestess, Priest, and Elders. And may the Curse of the Goddess be on any who do so.

SO BE IT ARDANE.

130. It is not forbidden to say as Christians do: "There be Witchcraft in the land," because our oppressors of old make it heresy not to believe in Witchcraft, and so a crime to deny it, which thereby puts you under suspicion.

131. But ever say "I know not of it here, perchance there may be, but afar off—I know not where."

132. But ever speak of those as old crones, consorting with the Devil and riding through the air.

133. But ever say: "But how many men may ride through the air an they be not light as thistledown?"

134. But the Curse of the Goddess be on any who cast any suspicion on any of the Brotherhood.

135. Or who speaks of any real meeting place where any abide.

SO BE IT ARDANE.

136. Let the Craft keep books with the names of all herbs which are good for men, and all cures, so all may learn.

137. But keep another book with all the Bales and Apies and let only the Elders and other trustworthy people have this knowledge.

SO BE IT ARDANE.

138. Remember the Art is the secret of the Gods and only may be used in earnest and never for show or pride, or vainglory.

139. Magicians and Christians may taunt us saying, "You have no power. Do magic before our eyes. Then only will we believe." Seeking to cause us to betray our Art before them.

140. Heed them not. For the Art is holy, and may only be used in need. And the Curse of the Gods be on any who break this Law.

SO BE IT ARDANE.

141. It ever be the way with women, and with men also that they ever seek new love.

142. Nor should we reprove them for this.

143. But it may be found to the disadvantage of the Craft.

144. As, so many a time it has happened that a High Priest or High Priestess impelled by love, hath departed with their love; that is, they have left the Coven.

145. Now if a High Priestess wishes to resign, they may do so in full Coven.

146. And this resignation is valid.

147. But if they should run off without resignation, who may know if they may not return within a few months?

148. So the Law is: If a High Priestess leaves her Coven, but returns within the space of a year and a day, then she shall be taken back and all shall be as before.

149. Meanwhile, if she has a deputy, that deputy shall act as High Priestess for as long as the High Priestess is away.

150. If she returns not at the end of a year and a day, then shall the Coven elect a new High Priestess.

151. Unless there be a good reason to the contrary, the person who has done the work should reap the benefit of the reward.

152. If somebody else is elected, the deputy is made maiden and deputy of the High Priestess.

SO BE IT ARDANE.

153. It hath been found that practicing the Art doth cause a fondness between aspirant and tutor, and it is the cause of better results if this be so.

154. But if for any reason this be undesirable, it can easily be avoided by both persons from the outset firmly resolving in their minds that if any such ensue, it shall be that of brother and sister, or parent and child.

155. And it is for this reason that a man may be taught by a woman and a woman by a man and that woman and woman and man and man should never attempt these practices together.

156. And may all the Curses of the Mighty Ones be on any who make such an attempt.

SO BE IT ARDANE.

157. Order and discipline must be kept.

158. A High Priestess or a High Priest may and should punish all faults.

159. To this end: all the Craft must receive their correction willingly.

160. All, properly prepared, the culprit kneeling, should be told his fault, and his sentence pronounced.

161. Punishment should be the $ followed by something amusing such as several S S S S, or something of this nature.

162. The culprit must acknowledge the justice of the punishment by kissing the hand of the Priestess and by kissing the $ on receiving sentence; and again thanking for punishment received.

SO BE IT ARDANE.

2

The Rituals

To Open the Circle

Let all be clean before the Gods. Being properly prepared, purify each other with Scourge or Cord: 3, 7, 9, 21 = 40. Give kiss. High Priest lights two white candles and places on Altar. Then place a white candle on each cardinal point of the Magic Circle.

Purify water and salt. First place point of Athame in water with right hand. Pronounce:

> *I exorcise Thee, O Creature of water, that though*
> *cast out from Thee all the impurities and*
> *uncleanlinesses of the Spirits of Phantasm. In the*
> *names of Arida and Kernunnos.*

Touching salt with Athame, pronounce:

> *Blessings be upon Thee, O Creature of salt. Let all*
> *malignity and hindrance pass henceforth and let all*
> *good enter in (but ever are we mindful that as water*
> *purifies the body so the salt purifies the soul).*
> *Wherefore do I bless Thee in the names of Arida*
> *and Kernunnos, that Thou mayest aid me.*

Then transfer three measures of salt with tip of Athame into the water and stir in clockwise direction three times. The Athame is now ready and purified.

Draw a nine-foot Magic Circle (or smaller or larger) as required with Athame, commencing in the East and ending in the East. The circle must be cut in an unbroken line. Then return to Altar facing North.

Take up water with right hand, transfer to left hand. Go to the East and sprinkle (asperge) with fingers in the East, South, West, and North, finish in the East. Return to Altar.

Take up incense and Censer in right hand. Repeat motions, censing Circle as before. Return to Altar.

The celebrants then anoint the opposite sex with water and salt in the 1, 2, 3, triangle and censes likewise.

Take a bell in right hand. Place in left hand, take Athame in right hand. Go to the East and salute in the following manner: Athame to lips, straight out above eye level, back to lips, then to right side down, with outstretched arm, and back to "carry" position before the right breast.

Cut large clear Pentacle, then pronounce:

> *Hear Ye, O Mighty Ones, Dread Lords of the*
> *Watchtowers of the East. I* (your name), *Priestess*
> *and Witch, do summon you, and I do command*
> *your presence at this our meeting, that our Circle be*
> *guarded and our rites be witnessed.*

Strike bell with Athame once in the East, South, West, and North. Finally giving salute only in the East. All present salute. The Circle is now perfect.

Dance around the Circle. High Priestess leading chanting of the ancient call. Dance and chant. Open Circle with ancient chant:

> *EKO EKO AZARAK,*
> *EKO EKO ZOMELEK,*
> *EKO EKO ARIDA,*
> *EKO EKO KERNUNNOS,*
> *BEZABI, LACHA, BACHABABA.*
> *LAMACH, CAHI, ACHABABA,*
> *KARRELOS, CAHI, ACHABABA,*
> *LAMACH LAMACH BACHAROUS,*

CARBAHAJI, SABALYOS,
BARYLOS.
LAZOS, ATHAME, CALYOLAS,
SAMAHAC, ET FAMYOLAS,
HARRAHYA!

If there is Coven Work to be done, now is the proper time to do it. To close or dismiss the Magic Circle. High Priestess/Priest, with ATHAME, goes to the East, salute. Then all present salute. Then celebrant or High Priestess says:

Hear Ye, O Mighty Ones. We thank you for your
attendance, and ere Ye depart to your lovely realms,
we bid you Hail and Farewell.

All present repeat *"Hail and Farewell"* and point Athames high. Repeat at other quarters, South, West, North, and finishing in the East. Give final salute.

Initiation of the First Degree

The Circle is cast in the usual manner. All except High Priestess, High Priest, and Handmaiden will leave the Circle. The initiate, having been ritually washed and blindfolded, is led in naked.

High Priestess or High Priest takes Athame or Sword and cuts doorway perfectly in Northeast and places tip of weapon at heart of postulant and says:

> *O thou who standeth on the threshold of pleant,*
> *world of men, and the domains of the Dread Lords*
> *of the outer spaces, hast Thou the courage to make*
> *the essay?*

Postulant:

> *I have.*

High Priestess:

> *For I say verily, it were better to rush upon my*
> *weapon and perish than to make the attempt with*
> *fear in thy heart.*

Postulant:

> *I have two passwords.*

High Priestess:

> *What are the two passwords?*

Postulant:

> *Perfect love and perfect peace.*

High Priestess (drops weapon and says):

> *All who bring such words are doubly welcome.*

High Priestess (she closes Circle and places weapon on Altar, goes behind postulant; puts left arm around waist, pulls postulant's head around over right shoulder, with right arm, and kisses lips and says):

> *I give you a third password—a kiss.*

High Priestess pushes postulant into Circle with her body and releasing postulant says:

This is the way all are first brought into the Circle.

She then leads Postulant sunwise to the South of the Altar and says:

O Thou who hast declared intent to become one of us, hear then that which thou must know to do. Single is the race, single of men and of Gods, from a single source we both draw breath, but a difference of power in everything keeps us apart, for we are as nothing, but the Gods stay forever. Yet we can, in greatness of minds, be like the Gods. Though we know not to what goal by day or in the night. Fate has written that we shall run beyond all seas, and earth's last boundaries, beyond the Spring of night and the Heavens' vast expanse there lies a majesty which is the domain of the Gods. Those who would pass through the Gates of Night and Day to that sweet place, which is between the world of men and the domains of the Lords of the outer spaces. Know that unless there is truth in thy heart, thy every effort is doomed to failure. HEAR THEN THE LAW. That Thou lovest all things in nature. That thou shalt suffer no person to be harmed by thy hands or in thy mind. That thou walkest humbly in the ways of men and the ways of the Gods. Also it is the Law that contentment thou shalt learn, through suffering, and from long years and from nobility of mind and of purpose. FOR THE WISE NEVER GROW OLD. Their minds are nourished by living in the daylight of the Gods and if among the vulgar some discoveries should arise concerning some maxims of thy belief in the Gods, so do thou, for the

*most part, keep silent. For there is a great risk that
thou straightway vomit up that which thou hast not
digested and when someone shall say to thee, thou
knowest naught and it bites thee not, then knowest
thou that thou hast begun the work, and as sheep
do not bring their food to the Shepherd to show how
much they have eaten, but digesting inwardly their
provender, bear outwardly wool and milk. Even so,
do not thou display the maxims to the vulgar, but
rather the works that flow when they are digested.
Now there is the ordeal.*

High Priestess takes stout Cord, ties Cord around postulant's right ankle, leaving ends free, and says:

Feet neither bound nor free.

High Priestess takes longer Cord and ties wrists behind back, then bringing Cord around neck and tying in the front. Taking Cord in the left hand with Athame in right, leads postulant sunwise and pointing Athame high with arm outstretched, says:

*Take heed O Lords of the Watchtowers of the East
that* (initiate) *properly prepared will be made
Priest/Priestess and Witch.*

She repeats this at the South, West, North, returning to the East salutes, returning with postulant to South of the Altar. Clasping postulant around body with left arm, runs Deosil three times around the Altar.

High Priestess says to Postulant:

Kneel.

High Priestess strikes eleven strokes on the bell and says to the postulant:

*Rise. In other religions the postulant kneels as
the Priest claims supreme power, but in the Art
Magical, we are taught to be humble, and we kneel*

and we say: Blessed are thy feet, that have brought
thee in thy ways. (kiss feet); *Blessed be thy knees,*
that shall kneel at the sacred Altar. (kiss knees);
Blessed be thy groins (womb if female) *without*
which we would not be. (kiss groins); *Blessed be thy*
breasts (if female), *erected in beauty and in*
strength. (kiss breasts); *Blessed be thy lips, which*
shall utter the sacred names. (kiss lips).

Take measure with a reel of white cotton [Cord]:
Around Head—tie a knot.
Around Breast—tie a knot.
Around Hips—tie a knot.
The Height—tie a knot.
Then break cotton and roll up around the finger. With needle or pin, prick thumb, catching blood on measure. Place measure on Altar. Make postulant kneel. Tie both feet together with Cord already around the ankles. Then attach Cord to the Altar. Strike bell three times with Athame and say:
High Priestess:

Art ready to swear thou wilt always be true to the
art?

Postulant:

Yes.

High Priestess strikes seven times on bell with Athame and says:

Thou must first be purified.

Take Scourge and strike postulant's bottom 3, 7, 9, 21 times (40 times in all); then High Priestess says:

Art always ready to protect, help, and defend thy
Brothers and Sisters of the Art?

Postulant:

Yes.

High Priestess:

> *Then say after me: I* (postulant's name), *in the*
> *presence of the Mighty Ones, do of my own free will*
> *and accord, most solemnly swear, without any*
> *reservation in me whatsoever, that I will ever keep*
> *secret and never reveal the secrets of the Arts, except*
> *it be to a person properly prepared, within such a*
> *Circle as I am now in, and that I will never deny the*
> *secrets to such a person if they be properly vouched*
> *for by a Brother or Sister of the Art. All this do I*
> *swear by my hopes of a future life. Mindful that my*
> *measure has been taken, and may my weapons turn*
> *against me if I break this my solemn oath.*

Loosen Cords from ankles, then Cord from Altar, leaving hands
bound. Remove blindfold, then assist postulant in rising up.
High Priestess:

> *I hereby consecrate thee with oil* (making sign with
> oil of the First Degree). *I hereby consecrate thee*
> *with wine* (making sign with wine of the First
> Degree). *I hereby consecrate thee with water*
> (making sign of the First Degree with water). *I*
> *hereby consecrate thee with fire* (making sign with
> incense of First Degree). *I hereby consecrate thee*
> *with my lips, Priest* (or Priestess) *and Witch*
> (making sign of the First Degree with a kiss).

She unties hands and says:

> *Now I present you with the working tools of the*
> *Witch. First, the Magic Sword, with this and with*
> *the Athame, thou canst form all Magic Circles.*
> *Subdue and punish all rebellious Spirits and*
> *Demons, and even persuade the evil Genii. With*
> *this in your hand, Thou art ruler of the Magic*
> *Circle* (kiss). *Next I present the Athame. This is the*

true Witches' weapon and it has all the powers of
the Magic Sword (kiss). Next I present the white-
handled Knife. Its use is to form all instruments
used in the Art. It can only be used within a Magic
Circle (kiss). Next I present the Magic Wand. Its use
is to control properly certain Genii to whom it
would not be mete to use the Magic Sword or
Athame (kiss). Next I present the Pentacle. This is
for the purpose of calling up the appropriate Spirits
(kiss). Next I present the Censer of incense. This is
used to encourage and welcome good Spirits and to
banish evil Spirits (kiss). Next I present the
Scourge. This is a sign of power and domination. It
is also used to cause suffering and purification. For
it is written, "To learn thou must suffer and be
purified." Art thou willing to suffer to learn?

Postulant:

I am (kiss).

High Priestess:

Next and lastly, I present the Cords. They are of use
to bind the Sigils of the Art—the material basis.
Also they are necessary in the oath and to enforce
thy will (kiss). I now salute you in the names of
Arida and Kernunnos newly made Priest/Priestess
and Witch.

High Priestess then leads postulant to the East. Salutes with Athame and proclaims:

Hear Ye, O Mighty Ones. (Name of witch) *has*
been consecrated a Priest/High Priestess of the Art
and a Brother/Sister of the Wicca.

This is repeated at the South, West, North, and finishing with salute at the East then returns to the Altar.

The Quaich (drinking horn, glass, or cup) is filled with wine. Others present then enter the Circle through the doorway cut by High Priestess or High Priest. New Witch is presented to Coven members. The Quaich is passed around the Circle, where all drink, then give it back to the High Priestess, who drains it. Postulant can be asked to relate any psychic experiences and can be shown the circle dance. Finish with *Cakes and Wine ceremony* which will follow, and a feast in Circle before closing (or after closing Circle). Feasting and dancing are permitted in Circle but I feel this should be done after closing the working Circle.

Elevation to the Second Degree

Form a circle. The Initiate must be properly prepared and bound. All are purified, including the Initiate. High Priestess/High Priest proclaims at the four quarters.

High Priestess:

> *Hear ye, Ye Mighty Ones.* (Initiate's witch name),
> *a duly consecrated Priestess/Priest and Witch is now*
> *properly prepared to be elevated to the Second*
> *Degree.*

High Priestess circles with Initiate three times with dance step. Initiate now kneels at the Altar and is secured at hands and feet. High Priestess/High Priest says:

> *To attain this degree it is necessary to be purified.*
> *Art willing to suffer to learn?*

Initiate:

> *I am.*

High Priestess/High Priest says:

> *I purify thee to take this oath rightly.*

High Priestess strikes three on the bell. Scourges 3, 7, 9, 21 then says:

> *Repeat after me: I,* (initiate's witch name), *swear*
> *on my Mother's womb, and by my honor amongst*
> *men, and by my Brothers and Sisters of the Art, that*
> *I will never reveal any secrets of the Art, except it be*
> *to a worthy person properly prepared in the center*
> *of a Magic Circle, such as I am now in. This I swear*
> *by my past lives and by my hopes of future ones to*
> *come and I devote myself to utter destruction if I*
> *break this my solemn oath.*

High Priestess/High Priest kneels, places left hand under Initiate's knees and right hand on his/her head and says:

I will all my power into thee.

Loosens Cords from Altar and ankles and assists Initiate to rise.
The consecration now follows.

High Priestess/High Priest makes the Pentagram on the genitals,
right foot, left knee, right knee, left foot, genitals, and says:

> *I consecrate Thee with oil* (kiss).
> *I consecrate Thee with Wine* (kiss).
> *I consecrate Thee with Water* (kiss).
> *1 consecrate Thee with fire* (kiss).
> *I consecrate Thee with my lips* (kiss).

Unbind hands, then present tools to Initiate.
High Priestess/High Priest:

> *You will now use the tools in turn. First the Magic
> Sword—redraw the Magic Circle.*

Initiate does this, then hands back tool to High Priest who gives
it a kiss.
High Priestess:

> *Second, the Athame—redraw the Magic Circle.*

Initiate does this, then hands back tool to High Priestess who
gives it a kiss.
High Priestess:

> *Third, the White-handled Knife—inscribe a Penta-
> gram on a candle.*

Initiate does this, then hands back tool to High Priestess who
gives it a kiss.
High Priestess:

> *Fourth, the Wand—wave to the Four Quarters.*

Initiate does this, then hands back tool to High Priestess who
gives it a kiss.
High Priestess:

> *Fifth, the Pentacle—show to the Four Quarters.*

Initiate does this, then hands back tool to High Priestess who gives it a kiss.

High Priestess:

> *Sixth, the Censer—cense the Circle.*

Initiate does this, then hands back tool to High Priestess who gives it a kiss.

High Priestess:

> *Seventh, the Cords—bind the High Priestess/High Priest.*

Initiate does this and High Priestess/High Priest gives a kiss. High Priestess says:

> *Learn that in Witchcraft thou must ever return triple. As I scourge thee, thou must scourge me, but triple. Where I gave thee three strokes, return nine; seven strokes, return twenty-one; nine strokes, return twenty-seven; twenty-one strokes, return sixty-three. That is 120 strokes in all. Take up the Scourge.*

Initiate does so and purifies the High Priestess with 120 strokes, then unbinds High Priestess/High Priest who gives a kiss. High Priestess/High Priest then says:

> *Thou hast obeyed the Law but mark well, when thou receiveth good, so equally art thou bound to return good threefold.*

The Initiate is then presented to the Four Quarters.
High Priestess/High Priest says:

> *Hail Ye, Mighty Ones, take heed that* (name of initiate) *hath been duly raised to the Second Degree.*

Finally salute East as usual. Return to center and finish.

Note: Only Second Degree Witches should attend at this stage of elevation.

Initiation of the Third Degree

High Priest, High Priestess, and Third Degree Witches only attend. In the absence of sufficient Initiates, use the people who are being instructed to enact after describing the Saga.

The High Priestess and High Priest are doubly purified. Others purified in usual manner. Circle is opened in the usual way. Initiates sit in cross-legged position around the Circle. Magus or High Priestess then says:

> *Having learned thus far, you must know why*
> *the Wicca are called "The Hidden Children of the*
> *Goddess."*

Then the Legend of the Goddess is narrated or enacted by High Priestess and High Priest. The High Priestess takes off her necklace and lays it on the Altar. She then puts on a veil and jewelry. The High Priest who is taking the part of the God is invested with a Horned Crown and girds on a Sword which he draws and stands in the God position with a Sword and a Scourge by the Altar. High Priestess meantime has left the Circle and stands outside in veil, etc.

The narrator, who must be a Third-Degree Witch or one of the Initiates, says:

> *In Ancient time, Our Lord, The Great Horned One,*
> *was as He still is, The Consoler, The Comforter, but*
> *men knew him as the Dread Lord of the Shadows—*
> *lonely—stern and just, but Our Lady, The Goddess,*
> *would solve all mysteries—even the mystery of*
> *Death. And so She journeyed to the Nether Lands,*
> *The Guardian of the Portal challenged her.*

The High Priestess taking the part of the Goddess advances to the Side of the Magic Circle. The Guardian (whoever is taking the part of the Guardian, and it can be the Narrator) challenges her with the Sword or Athame.

Guardian of the Portal says:

> *Strip off thy garments, lay aside thy jewels, for*
> *naught may ye bring with thee into this our land.*

Narrator:

> *So she laid down her garments and her jewels and*
> *was bound as all living must be who seek to enter*
> *the realms of Death, The Mighty Ones.*

The High Priestess takes off the veil and jewelry, and lays them down outside the Circle. The Guardian of the Portal binds her with Cords and brings her inside the Circle.

Narrator:

> *Such was her beauty that Death himself knelt and*
> *laid his Sword and Crown at her feet and kissed*
> *her feet.*

The High Priest comes forward and gazes at her, and He lays the Horned Crown and the Sword at the feet of the High Priestess and kisses her feet. High Priest and High Priestess repeat words after spoken by narrator.

Narrator:

> *Blessed are thy feet that have brought thee in these*
> *ways. Abide with me, but let me place my cold hand*
> *on thy heart.* (High Priest repeats.)

Narrator:

> *And she replied, "I love thee not."* (High Priestess
> repeats.)

Narrator:

> *Why dost thou cause all things that I love and take*
> *delight in, to fade and die?* (High Priestess
> repeats.)

Narrator:

> *"Lady," replied Death, "'Tis age and fate, against*
> *which I am helpless. Age causes all things to wither,*
> *but when men die, at the end of time, I give them*
> *rest and strength so that they may return. But you,*

you are lovely. Return not: abide with me." (High
Priest repeats.)

Narrator:

But she answers, "I love thee not." (High Priestess
repeats.)

Narrator:

*"Then," said Death, "An you receive not my hand
on your heart, you must kneel at Death's Scourge."*

High Priest repeats, then he rises and takes up the Scourge from
the Altar.

Narrator:

"It is fate, better so," she replied. (High Priestess
repeats.) *And she knelt.*

The High Priestess kneels before the Altar and the High Priest
uses the Scourge 3, 7, 9, 21 = 40 times.

Narrator:

*And Death scourged her tenderly, and she cried, "I
knew the pangs of love."* (High Priestess repeats.)

Narrator:

*And Death raised her and said, "Blessed Be." And
gave her the fivefold kiss saying, "Thus only may
you attain to joy and knowledge."*

High Priest repeats, and then raises the High Priestess and gives
her the fivefold kiss and unfastens her cords.

Narrator:

*And he taught her all the mysteries, and he gave her
the necklace which is the circle of rebirth.*

High Priest takes High Priestess' necklace from the Altar and
replaces it about her neck. The High Priestess takes up the Sword
and Horned Crown from the floor where the High Priest placed

them, and gives them back to him. Then he stands as before, by the Altar, in the position of the God and she stands by his side in the Pentacle position of the Goddess.

Narrator:

> *And she taught him the mystery of the sacred cup which is the cauldron of rebirth. They loved and were one, for there be three great mysteries in the life of man. Magic (love) controls them all. For to fulfill love, you must return again at the same time, and at the same place, as the loved one, and you must meet, and know and remember and love them again. But to be reborn, you must die, and be made ready for a new body, and to die you must be born, and without love, you may not be born. And our Goddess ever inclineth to love and mirth and happiness and guardeth and cherisheth Her hidden children in life: And in death She teacheth the way to have communion, and even in the world, She teacheth them the Mystery of the Magic Circle, which is placed between the worlds.*

The High Priestess and High Priest then replace the Scourge, and the Sword, Crown, and etc. upon the Altar. The High Priestess and High Priest then invite the Initiates to ask questions on the Legend of the Goddess, which must be answered truthfully and also explain the symbolism contained in the Legend, including the Great Rite. Cakes and wine follow.

The Circle is closed.

The Great Rite

In ancient times the Great Rite was practiced, but I do not know of any Witches in America or England who still practice the Great Rite. You may reject it, or if you feel closer to the Gods by returning as much as possible to the worship of the Ancients, then by all means do it.

THE GREAT RITE—at the end of each Sabbat Rite, the ancient ones had to "Earth" the power that had been raised within the Circle so that the power raised would not remain in the atmosphere afterwards. They earthed the power by committing the "Sex Act," which brought them down from the mystical to the material level. Each Sabbat Rite ended with this act and it was called "The Great Rite."

The Great Rite is performed as an act of worship to the God and Goddess. Obviously, if everybody indulged in lovemaking at the end of the rite, within the Magic Circle, it would look as if an orgy were taking place. Mostly the coveners did this in private after leaving the Magic Circle. Sex Magic is one of the most powerful of all acts of Magic and not to be taken lightly, and certainly I believe should be performed in private before the Gods.

The Charge of the Goddess

Listen to the words of the Great Mother, who was of old, called amongst men, Artemis, Astarte, Dione, Melusine, Aphrodite, Cerridwen, Diana, Arionhod, Bride, and by many other names.

At mine Altar, the youths of Lacedemon in Sparta made due sacrifice. Whenever ye have need of anything, once in the month and better it be when the Moon is Full, then shall ye assemble in some secret place and adore the Spirit of Me, who am Queen of all the Witcheries. There shall ye assemble, who are feign to learn all sorceries who have not as yet won my deepest secrets. To these will I teach that which is as yet unknown. And ye shall be free from all slavery and as a sign that ye be really free, ye shall be naked in your rites and ye shall sing, feast, make music and love, all in my presence. For mine is the ecstasy of the Spirit and mine is also joy on earth. For my Law is love unto all beings. Keep pure your highest ideals, strive ever towards them. Let none stop you or turn you aside. For mine is the secret that opens upon the door of youth and mine is the Cup of the Wine of Life and the Cauldron of Cerridwen, which is the Holy Grail of Immortality. I am the Gracious Goddess who gives the gift of joy unto the heart of man upon earth. I give the knowledge of the Spirit Eternal, and beyond death I give peace and freedom and reunion with those that have gone before. Nor do I demand aught or sacrifice, for behold I am the Mother of all things, and my love is poured out upon the earth.

Hear ye the words of the Star Goddess. She, in the dust of whose feet are the Hosts of Heaven, whose body encircleth the universe.

I who am the beauty of the Green Earth, and the White Moon amongst the stars and the mystery of the Waters, and the desire of the heart of man, I call unto thy soul to arise and come unto me. For I am the Soul of Nature who giveth life to the universe; from me all things proceed and unto me all things must return. Beloved of the Gods and men, whose innermost divine self shall be enfolded in the raptures of the Infinite, let my worship be in the heart. Rejoiceth, for behold, all acts of love and pleasure are my rituals; therefore, let there be beauty and strength—power and compassion— honor and humility, mirth and reverence—within you. And thou who thinkest to seek me, know that thy seeking and yearning avail thee not unless thou knowest the mystery, that if that which thou seekest thou findeth not within thyself, thou wilt never find it without thee. For behold—I have been with thee from the beginning, and I am that which is attained at the end of desire.

Invocation to the Horned God

By the flame that burneth bright,
O Horned One!
We call Thy name into the night,
O Ancient One!
Thee we invoke, by the Moon-led sea,
By the standing stone and the twisted tree.
Thee we invoke, where gather Thine own,
By the nameless shore, forgotten and lone.
Come where the round of the dance is trod,
Horn and Hoof of the Goat Foot God!
By moonlit meadow, on dusky hill,
When the haunted wood is hushed and still,
Come to the charm of the chanted prayer,
As the Moon bewitches the midnight air.
Evoke Thy powers that potent bide,
In shining stream and the secret tide.
In fiery flame by starlight pale,
In shadowy host that rides the gale.
And by the ferndrakes, fairy haunted,
Of forests wild and woods enchanted,
Come? O Come!
To the Heart-beat's drum!
Come to us who gather below,
When the broad white Moon is climbing slow.
Through the stars to the heavens' height,
We hear Thy hoofs on the wind of night!
As black tree branches shake and sigh,
By joy and terror we know Thee nigh.
We speak the spell Thy power unlocks,
At Solstice, Sabbat, and Equinox!

Ceremony of the Blessing of Cakes and Wine

High Priestess stands in the God position. Feet are together, arms crossed under breasts, the Athame in right hand, the Scourge in the left hand. High Priest kisses her feet, then knees, then kneels with head below High Priestess' knees and adores.

High Priest fills Quaich and offers to the High Priestess who, holding Athame between the palms, places the point in the cup and says:

High Priestess:

> *As the Athame is the male, so the Cup is the female*
> *and enjoined they bring happiness.*

High Priestess lays Athame aside and drinks from Cup and passes to all coveners. Each drinks. The Cup returns to the High Priestess, Who drains the Cup. High Priest presents cakes on Pentacle to the High Priestess who blesses with Athame. High Priest lifts cakes on Pentacle and says:

> *O Queen, most secret, Bless this food unto our bod-*
> *ies, bestowing wealth, strength, joy, and peace, and*
> *that fulfillment of love which is perpetual*
> *happiness.*

The High Priest again presents the cakes to the High Priestess, Who eats while the High Priest again offers Her the Cup. All present sit and the High Priest invites the High Priestess to join them. The Paten of cakes and the Cup of Wine is passed to all present.

Witches' Chant

Darksome night and shining Moon,
Hearken to the Witches' rune.
East then South, West then North,
Hear! Come! I call Thee forth!

By all the powers of land and sea,
Be obedient unto me.
Wand and Pentacle and Sword,
Hearken ye unto my word.

Cords and Censer, Scourge and Knife,
Waken all ye into life.
Powers of the Witches' Blade,
Come ye as the charge is made.

Queen of Heaven, Queen of Hell,
Send your aid unto the spell.
Horned Hunter of the night,
Work my will by magic rite.

By all the powers of land and sea,
As I do say, "So mote it be."
By all the might of Moon and Sun,
As I do will, it shall be done.

Incantation

ENOS, ARIDA JUVATE
ENOS, ARIDA JUVATE
ENOS, ARIDA JUVATE
NEVE, LUERVE, KERNUNNOS
NEVE, LUERVE, KERNUNNOS
NEVE, LUERVE, KERNUNNOS
SINS INCURRERE IN PLEORES
SINS INCURRERE IN PLEORES
SINS INCURRERE IN PLEORES
SATUR FU FERE DIANUS
SATUR FU FERE DIANUS
SATUR FU FERE DIANUS
LINEN SALI STA BERBER
LINEN SALI STA BERBER
LINEN SALI STA BERBER
TRIUMPHE
TRIUMPHE
TRIUMPHE
SEMUNIS ALTERNIE ADVOCAPITO
SEMUNIS ALTERNIE ADVOCAPITO
SEMUNIS ALTERNIE ADVOCAPITO
CONCTOS
CONCTOS
CONCTOS

Drawing Down the Moon

This ceremony can be performed when holding Esbats at Full Moon or when Moon is waxing. High Priestess or High Priest casts the Circle. Coveners are properly prepared and purified. High Priestess assumes Goddess position.

High Priest draws down the Moon on either High Priestess or Handmaiden. A period of silence usually follows for many things may happen when this is done for it is a very powerful ceremony.

The High Priest will stand before the High Priestess, who is in the Osiris or God position, and the High Priest will say:

> *I invoke Thee and call upon Thee, O Mighty*
> *Mother of us all. Bringer of Fruitfulness by seed and*
> *by root. I invoke Thee, by stem and by bud. I invoke*
> *Thee, by life and by love and call upon Thee to*
> *descend into the body of this Thy Priestess and*
> *Servant. Hear with her ears, speak with her tongue,*
> *touch with her hands, kiss with her lips, that thy*
> *servants may be fulfilled.*

The High Priestess then adopts the Goddess position and the High Priest draws down the power by the force of his concentration and prayer, touching her on the breast and womb with the Wand. He then kneels at her feet and adores while concentrating. The High Priestess shall then recite The Charge.

> *All ye assembled at mine shrine,*
> *Mother Darksome and Divine.*
> *Mine the Scourge and mine the Kiss,*
> *Here I charge you in this sign.*

Assumes God position.

> *All ye assembled in my sight,*
> *Bow before my spirit bright.*

Coveners bow before High Priestess.

> *Aphrodite, Arionhod,*
> *Lover of the Horned God,*

Mighty Queen of Witchery and night,
Morgan, Etoine, Nisene,
Diana, Bridgid, Melusine,
Am I named of old by men,
Artemis and Cerridwen,
Hell's dark mistress, Heaven's queen.
Ye who would ask of me a rune,
Or who would ask of me a boon,
Meet me in some secret glade
Dance my round in greenwood shade,
By the light of the Full Moon.
In a place, wild and lone,
Dance about mine altar stone;
Work my holy mystery.
Ye who are feign to sorcery,
I bring ye secrets yet unknown.
No more shall ye know slavery,
Who give true worship unto me.
Ye who tread my round on Sabbat night,
Come ye all naked to the rite,
In token that ye be really free.
I teach ye the mystery of rebirth,
Work ye my mysteries in mirth.
Heart joined to heart and lip to lip,
Five are the points of fellowship,
That bring ye ecstasy on earth,
For I am the circle of rebirth.
I ask no sacrifice, but do bow,
No other Law but love I know,
By naught but love may I be known.
All things living are mine own,
From me they come, to me they go.

Close and dismiss Circle.

Ancient Wiccan Grace

Answer us, O Ancient Horned One,
Provender and power are Thine.
Hear and answer, Gracious Goddess,
Grant us laughter, wit and wine,
Descend on us, O Thou of blessings,
Come among us, make us glad.
Since Thou art Chief of our creation,
Why, O Why should we be sad?
Beam on us, O joyous Bacchus,
Banish heavy-hearted hate.
Accept our Craft, O Greatest Mother,
Let cheerful brightness be our fate.
SO MOTE IT BE!

Ancient Runic Spell

Upon this Candle I will write,
What I receive of Thee this night.
Grant what I wish You to do,
I dedicate this Rite to You.
I trust that You will grant this Boon,
O Lovely Goddess, of the Moon.

I call Earth to bond my Spell
Air speed its travel well,
Fire give It Spirit from Above,
Water quench my Spell with Love.

To Consecrate All Your
Ritual Instruments

High Priest or High Priestess casts the Magic Circle. All attending must be properly prepared and purified. High Priest or High Priestess faces the Altar in North. Coveners form circle and each holds in his strongest hand the tools he is consecrating. High Priest or High Priestess anoints all ritual instruments being held by coveners.

High Priest or High Priestess invokes the Watchers to bear witness as the instruments are consecrated to the Craft.

High Priestess:

> *Coveners! In your words and by the force of your*
> *will power and imagination, charge your* (name of
> tool) *concentrating on the purpose you wish the*
> (name of tool) *to serve.*

> *Grasp the* (name of tool) *in your strongest hand*
> *and concentrate your will power into the* (name of
> tool).

> *Concentrate your desire into the* (tool), *that its*
> *power will increase with each new day. That its*
> (name of tool) *power will last as long as the* (tool)
> *itself. That Ghosts, Spirits, human beings, and*
> *animals are to obey your will. That they will obey*
> *your magic* (name the tool) *whether in the physical*
> *world or on the Astral* (spiritual) *or Mental plane.*

> *Charge your* (name the tool) *to work on dead*
> *material also.*

> *Concentrate on the Universal God Force* (Akasha
> principle) *and draw down this Life Force from the*
> *Great Universal God Force into your* (tool).

> *Charge your* (name the tool) *with the knowledge*
> *that the Life Force Power in the* (tool) *will*
> *automatically intensify from one day to the next.*

Charge your (tool) *to automatically, without any effort on your part, bring a piece of Life Force from the Universal Life Force, which will then radiate from your* (tool) *whenever and to whatever it is needed.*

This force or power in your (name of tool) *can be used for the good of yourself and for others as you wish, or if necessary it may be used against your enemies.*

SO MOTE IT BE.

3

The Sabbats

Our belief that the Moon being a physical manifestation of the power and glory of the Goddess, the Sabbat Rites are celebrated at midnight on the night before the day of the festival.

We have eight Great Sabbat Festivals and thirteen New Moon and thirteen Full Moon Esbats during the year. Our religious year begins with Yule. The Great Sabbats are:

> *Yule: December 21. The Winter Solstice. We celebrate the return or rebirth of the Sun.*
>
> *Candlemas: February 2. A fire festival. In olden times all new Witches were initiated at Candlemas, the "Feast of the Waxing Light."*
>
> *The Spring Rite: March 21. The Spring Equinox. The Celebration for fertility of man, crops, and animals.*
>
> *Rudemas: May 1. A fertility Sabbat.*
>
> *Beltane: June 21. Midsummer festival celebrating the Summer Solstice. Gather as many covens together as possible.*
>
> *Lammas: August 1. Rites for increase in material supply.*

Autumn Equinox Rite: September 21. A celebration of Thanksgiving for the blessings of the year, for food, clothing, and shelter.

Hallowmas: October 31. Celebration for the reunion of Souls of the family members who have left the physical plane. We can ask them to return on this night and give us messages of Wisdom.

I would have you remember that "there is a time and place for all things." Work out your own timetable, according to the phases of the Moon and the movement of the planets for the workings of the Craft. Remember the two sides (light and dark) of the Moon for casting spells. Be sure you have sufficient knowledge of astrology because if you do not heed the Moon's phases and the elemental power tides, your spell casting will avail you nothing.

It is to your benefit that you celebrate each Great Sabbat and the New Moon and Full Moon Esbats.

The Great Sabbats you are commanded to keep if you would retain your Witch power.

SO BE IT!

The Yule Sabbat

The Celebration of the Rebirth of the Sun
December 21

Let all be properly prepared and purified. High Priest casts the Magic Circle and invokes the Ancient Ones to bear witness. High Priest decorates the Altar (standing in the North of the Circle) with pine boughs, holly, ivy, and mistletoe. Two red candles, incense, oil, and the Sacred Tools of the Craft. A red candle is on the Altar for each covener present.

High Priest places the Cauldron of Keridwen in the center of the Magic Circle and encircles it with a wreath of pine boughs, holly, ivy, and mistletoe. High Priest lays the Balefire within the Cauldron with nine woods: rowan, apple, elder, holly, pine, cedar, juniper, poplar, and dogwood.

High Priestess stands in the West of the Magic Circle facing East and recites:

> *All ye assembled at mine shrine,*
> *Mother Darksome and Divine.*
> *Mine the Scourge and mine the Kiss*
> *Here I charge you in this sign.*

High Priestess assumes the Goddess position.

> *All ye assembled in my sight,*
> *Bow before my spirit bright.*

All coveners bow to High Priestess.

> *Aphrodite, Arionhod,*
> *Lover of the Horned God,*
> *Mighty Queen of Witchery and night,*
> *Morgan, Etoine, Nisene,*
> *Diana, Bridgid, Melusine,*
> *Am I named of old by men,*
> *Artemis and Cerridwen,*
> *Hell's dark mistress, Heaven's queen.*
> *Ye who would ask of me a rune,*

Or who would ask of me a boon,
Meet me in some secret glade,
Dance my round in greenwood shade,
By the light of the Full Moon.
In a place, wild and lone,
Dance about mine altar stone;
Work my holy mystery.
Ye who are feign to sorcery,
I bring ye secrets yet unknown.
No more shall ye know slavery,
Who give true worship unto me.
Ye who tread my round on Sabbat night,
Come Ye all naked to the rite,
In token that ye be really free.
I teach ye the mystery of rebirth,
Work ye my mysteries in mirth.
Heart joined to heart and lip to lip,
Five are the points of fellowship,
That bring ye ecstasy on earth,
For I am the circle of rebirth.
I ask no sacrifice, but do bow,
No other Law but love I know,
By naught but love may I be known.
All things living are mine own,
From me they come, to me they go.

The coveners have remained silent and standing inside the Magic Circle. High Priest kindles the fire of Keridwen by drawing down a spark of elemental fire from the Universal Source. High Priest passes to the East and bows. He returns to the Altar. High Priest assumes the Horned God position and recites Invocation:

By the flame that burneth bright,
O Horned One!
We call Thy name into the night,
O Ancient One.

Thee we invoke, by the Moon-led sea,
By the standing stone and the twisted tree.
Thee we invoke, where gather Thine own,
By the nameless shore, forgotten and lone.
Come where the round of the dance is trod,
Horn and Hoof of the Goat Foot God!
By moonlit meadow, on dusky hill,
When the haunted wood is hushed and still,
Come to the charm of the chanted prayer,
As the Moon bewitches the midnight air.
Evoke Thy powers that potent bide,
In shining stream and the secret tide.
In fiery flame by starlight pale,
In shadowy host that rides the gale.
And by the ferndrakes, fairy haunted,
Of forests wild and woods enchanted,
Come? O Come!
To the heart-beat's drum!
Come to us who gather below,
When the broad white Moon is climbing slow.
Through the stars to the heavens' height,
We hear Thy hoofs on the wind of night!
As black tree branches shake and sigh,
By joy and terror we know Thee nigh.
We speak the spell Thy power unlocks,
At Solstice, Sabbat, and Equinox!

The coveners file past, male then female. As they pass the High Priestess, the females curtsy and the males bow and kiss the right cheek of the High Priestess. As they pass the High Priest, he hands each one a red unlit taper from the Altar, which they light at the Cauldron and again form a circle line, alternately male-female.

High Priestess:

Queen of the Moon,
Queen of the Stars,
Queen of the Horns,

Queen of the Fires,
Queen of the Earth,
Bring to us the Child of Promise!
For it is the Great Mother
Who gives birth to Him;
It is the Lord of Life
Who is born again.
Darkness and tears are set aside,
When the Sun comes up again.
Golden Sun of hill and mountain,
Illumine the world,
Illumine the seas,
Illumine the rivers,
Illumine us all.
Grief be laid and joy be raised,
Blessed be the Great Mother!
Without beginning, without end,
Everlasting to Eternity.
Evoe! Io! Evoe! He!

At this point all raise their lighted tapers high and chant:

Evoe! Io! Evoe! He!
Blessed Be, Blessed Be.

High Priest leads the coveners in a dance around the High Priestess and the Altar chanting.
High Priest:

EKO EKO AZARAK,
EKO EKO ZOMELEK,
EKO EKO ARIDA,
EKO EKO KERNUNNOS,
BEZABI, LACHA, BACHABABA.
LAMACH, CAHI, ACHABABA,
KARRELOS, CAHI, ACHABABA,
LAMACH LAMACH BACHAROUS,

CARBAHAJI, SABALYOS,
BARYLOS.
LAZOS, ATHAME, CALYOLAS,
SAMAHAC, ET FAMYOLAS,
HARRAHYA!

When the *HARRAHYA!* is chanted the High Priest takes the High Priestess by the hand and leaps the Cauldron. Then each male takes a female by the hand and leaps over the Cauldron. He leaps and holds her hand while she leaps the Cauldron. As each leap is enacted, everyone shouts *"HARRAHYA!"*

High Priestess resumes the Goddess position. High Priest leads the coveners in a file past the High Priestess. As the High Priest passes the High Priestess, he bows and kisses her cheek, then resumes his position at Altar, facing East. Places lighted taper on the Altar in a holder provided for this purpose.

As the coveners pass the High Priestess, the females curtsy, the men bow to High Priestess and kiss her on the right cheek. (Kiss of fealty.) As the coveners pass the High Priest, they hand him their lighted tapers, which are placed on the Altar.

High Priestess holds the Chalice while the High Priest pours wine into the Chalice. She continues to hold the Chalice over the Cauldron of Keridwen as the High Priest picks up his Athame and plunges it into the Chalice of wine. High Priestess sips from the Chalice and passes the Chalice to the High Priest. He sips the wine and passes the Chalice to the coveners, who in turn sip from the Chalice. The cup returns to the High Priestess (completing the circle), who drains the wine. The High Priestess always finishes the wine in the cup.

High Priest and High Priestess and all coveners face North, East, South, and West and salute with Athames while the High Priest thanks the Ancient Ones and gives them license to depart the Circle.

Celebrate with cakes and wine and much feasting, dancing, and Brotherhood.

The Candlemas Sabbat

The Feast of the Waxing Light
February 2

Let all be properly prepared and purified. High Priest casts the Magic Circle and invokes the Ancient Ones. Altar is placed in the North of Circle and decorated with a wreath of white flowers. Two white altar candles and a white candle for each covener and the Sacred Altar tools. Cauldron placed in the center of the Circle contains the nine woods: rowan, apple, elder, holly, pine, cedar, juniper, poplar, and dogwood.

High Priest stands at Altar facing East. High Priestess enters Circle and stands in the West facing East. The coveners file into the Circle, male and female, and as they pass before the High Priestess the females curtsy and the males bow and give Her the Kiss of Fealty (right cheek). As they pass the High Priest, he hands each a white taper candle.

The High Priestess recites the Goddess Charge:

> *All ye assembled at mine shrine,*
> *Mother Darksome and Divine.*
> *Mine the Scourge and mine the Kiss,*
> *Here I charge you in this sign.*

Assumes the Goddess position.

> *All ye assembled in my sight,*
> *Bow before my spirit bright.*

Coveners bow before High Priestess.

> *Aphrodite, Arionhod,*
> *Lover of the Horned God,*
> *Mighty Queen of Witchery and night,*
> *Morgan, Etoine, Nisene,*
> *Diana, Bridgid, Melusine,*
> *Am I named of old by men,*
> *Artemis and Cerridwen,*

Hell's dark mistress, Heaven's queen.
Ye who would ask of me a rune,
Or who would ask of me a boon,
Meet me in some secret glade,
Dance my round in greenwood shade,
By the light of the Full Moon.
In a place, wild and lone,
Dance about mine altar stone;
Work my holy mystery.
Ye who are feign to sorcery,
I bring ye secrets yet unknown.
No more shall ye know slavery,
Who give true worship unto me.
Ye who tread my round on Sabbat night,
Come ye naked to the rite,
In token that ye be really free.
I teach ye the mystery of rebirth,
Work ye my mysteries in mirth.
Heart joined to heart and lip to lip,
Five are the points of fellowship,
That bring ye ecstasy on earth,
For I am the circle of rebirth.
I ask no sacrifice, but do bow,
No other Law but love I know
By naught but love may I be known.
All things living are mine own,
From me they come, to me they go.

High Priest lights two altar candles and incense. Picks up altar candle and lights the Cauldron fire. High Priest assumes the God position. He recites the Invocation to the Horned God:

By the flame that burneth bright,
O Horned One!
We call Thy name into the night,
O Ancient One!

Thee we invoke, by the Moon-led sea,
By the standing stone and the twisted tree.
Thee we invoke, where gather Thine own,
By the nameless shore, forgotten and lone.
Come where the round of the dance is trod,
Horn and Hoof of the Goat Foot God!
By Moonlit meadow, on dusky hill,
When the haunted wood is hushed and still,
Come to the charm of the chanted prayer,
As the Moon bewitches the midnight air.
Evoke Thy powers that potent bide,
In shining stream and the secret tide.
In fiery flame by starlight pale
In shadowy host that rides the gale.
And by the ferndrakes, fairy haunted,
Of forests wild and woods enchanted,
Come? O Come!
To the heart-beat's drum!
Come to us who gather below,
When the broad white moon is climbing slow.
Through the stars to the heavens' height,
We hear Thy hoofs on the wind of night!
As black tree branches shake and sigh,
By joy and terror we know Thee nigh.
We speak the spell Thy power unlocks,
At Solstice, Sabbat, and Equinox!

The High Priest leads the coveners in a spiral dance that winds inward to the Cauldron, where each lights their taper at the Cauldron. Then the spiral unwinds. As the spiral dance is performed the High Priest and coveners chant:

EKO EKO AZARAK,
EKO EKO ZOMELEK,
EKO EKO ARIDA,
EKO EKO KERNUNNOS,

BEZABI, LACHA, BACHABABA.
LAMACH, CAHI, ACHABABA,
KARRELOS, CAHI, ACHABABA,
LAMACH LAMACH BACHAROUS,
CARBAHAJI, SABALYOS,
BARYLOS.
LAZOS, ATHAME, CALYOLAS,
SAMAHAC ET FAMYOLAS,
HARRAHYA!

High Priest leads the coveners in a dance around the High
Priestess, Altar, Cauldron in a line just inside the Circle, chanting:

Darksome night and shining Moon,
Hearken to the Witches' rune.
East then South, West then North,
Here! Come! I call Thee forth.
By all the powers of land and sea,
Be obedient unto me.
Wand and Pentacle and sword,
Hearken ye unto my word.
Cords and Censer, Scourge and Knife,
Waken all ye into life.
Powers of the Witches' blade,
Come ye as the charge is made.
Queen of Heaven, Queen of Hell,
Send your aid into the spell.
Horned Hunter of the night,
Work my will by magic rite.
By all the powers of land and sea,
As I do say, "So mote it be."
By all the might of Moon and Sun,
As I do will, it shall be done.

End of chant and dance. High Priest and coveners salute, holding candles high. The High Priest says:

Behold the Great Mother
Who hath brought forth
The light of the world.
EKO EKO ARIDA,
EKO EKO KERNUNNOS.

Kiss. The Coveners pass their tapers to the High Priest at the Altar, who returns them to the Altar, where they remain lighted.

High Priest returns candle to Altar and coveners file past the High Priestess and curtsy and males bow and give kiss. High Priestess blesses the cakes and wine and the Chalice is passed. The paten of cakes is passed and each partakes.

High Priest and High Priestess and coveners face North, East, South, and West and salute while the High Priest thanks the Ancient Ones and gives them license to depart the Circle.

This being a feast of the Waxing light of the Sun, the singing, games, dancing, and feasting after the rite is performed, last through the night and until the Sun's rays shine forth on the horizon. Then all witches go forth to welcome the Sun by standing in the morning Sunlight in a Greeting of Welcome. As the Sun's rays fall upon each covener, they bow and say:

EKO EKO ARIDA,
EKO EKO KERNUNNOS.

The Spring Sabbat

The Vernal Equinox
March 21

Green candles at four quarters. Silver candles on Altar which is wreathed with spring flowers and a fire is prepared in the East within the Circle. High Priestess or High Priest casts the Circle. High Priestess should read The Charge with the coveners standing around the Circle alternately male-female.

> *All ye assembled at mine shrine,*
> *Mother Darksome and Divine.*
> *Mine the Scourge and mine the Kiss,*
> *Here I charge you in this sign.*

Assumes God position.

> *All ye assembled in my sight,*
> *Bow before my spirit bright.*

Coveners bow before High Priestess.

> *Aphrodite, Arionhod,*
> *Lover of the Horned God,*
> *Mighty Queen of Witchery and night,*
> *Morgan, Etoine, Nisene,*
> *Diana, Bridgid, Melusine,*
> *Am I named of old by men,*
> *Artemis and Cerridwen,*
> *Hell's dark mistress, Heaven's queen.*
> *Ye who would ask of me a rune,*
> *Or who would ask of me a boon,*
> *Meet me in some secret glade,*
> *Dance my round in greenwood shade,*
> *By the light of the Full Moon.*
> *In a place, wild and lone,*
> *Dance about mine altar stone;*
> *Work my holy mystery,*

Ye who are feign to sorcery,
I bring ye secrets yet unknown.
No more shall ye know slavery,
Who give true worship unto me.
Ye who tread my round on Sabbat night,
Come ye all naked to the rite,
In token that ye be really free.
I teach Ye the mystery of rebirth
Work ye my mysteries in mirth.
Heart joined to heart and lip to lip,
Five are the points of fellowship,
That bring ye ecstasy on earth,
For I am the circle of rebirth.
I ask no sacrifice, but do bow,
No other Law but love I know,
By naught but love may I be known,
All things living are mine own,
From me they come, to me they go.

High Priest stands in the East beside the unlit fire. High Priestess stands facing High Priest, holding Wand.

High Priestess:

We kindle this fire this day in the presence of the
Almighty Ones without malice, without jealousy,
without envy, without fear of ought beneath the Sun
but the High Gods. Thee we invoke, O Light of the
Fire, O That which is Life. Be Thou as a bright
flame before us, be Thou a smooth path between us,
be Thou a guiding star above, kindle though within
our hearts, a flame of love. For our neighbors, for
our foes, to our neighbors, to our foes, to our friends,
to our kindred all, to all men upon the broad earth.
O Merciful Son of Cerridwen, from the lowliest
thing that liveth, to the name that is Highest of all,
Kernunnos.

The High Priestess then draws the invoking Pentagram on the High Priest with her Wand, then hands it to him with a kiss. High Priest lights fire. High Priestess and High Priest then lead the coveners around the Altar, leaping the flames as they reach them, until the fire begins to die down.

The coveners resume their places around the Altar. High Priest pours wine into the Quaich and High Priestess drinks. The High Priest drinks and passes Quaich around to the coveners, each drinks, finishing with the High Priestess, who drains it. This can be followed by dancing and games, cakes and wine if desired. Close Circle. Feast follows.

The Rudemas Sabbat

May Eve

April 30

Place green candles at the four cardinal points in the Circle. Place two white candles on the Altar. Decorate with spring flowers. High Priestess or High Priest casts the Magic Circle. All coveners are doubly purified. Dance around the Circle with Besoms chanting:

> *O do not tell the Priests of our Arts*
> *For they would call it sin;*
> *For we will be in the woods all night,*
> *A-conjuring Summer in.*
> *And bring you good news by word of mouth,*
> *For women, cattle and corn;*
> *For the Sun is a-coming up from the South*
> *With Oak and Ash and Thorn.*

Do the meeting dance, chanting:

> *EKO EKO AZARAK,*
> *EKO EKO ZOMELEK,*
> *EKO EKO ARIDA*
> *EKO EKO KERNUNNOS,*
> *BEZABI, LACHA, BACHABABA.*
> *LAMACH, CAHI, ACHABABA,*
> *KARRELOS, CAHI, ACHABABA,*
> *LAMACH LAMACH BACHAROUS,*
> *CARBAHAJI, SABALYOS,*
> *BARYLOS.*
> *LAZOS, ATHAME, CALYOLAS,*
> *SAMAHAC, ET FAMYOLAS,*
> *HARRAHYA!*

High Priestess assumes the God position. High Priest invokes and draws down the Moon. High Priest, kneeling, invokes:

I invoke Thee and call upon Thee, O Mighty
Mother of us all, Bringer of all Fruitfulness, by seed
and by root, by stem and by bud, by leaf and flower
and fruit, by life and love, do I invoke Thee to
descend upon the body of Thy Servant and High
Priestess (name), *here.*

The sign of the 1, 2, 3 triangle is given to the High Priestess by all the men, all women bow. High Priest makes sign of the 1, 2, 3 triangle on High Priestess and concentrates his power upon her whilst kneeling at her feet and adoring.

All concentrate whilst High Priestess reads The Charge:

All ye assembled at mine shrine,
Mother Darksome and Divine.
Mine the Scourge and mine the Kiss,
Here I charge you in this sign.

Assumes God position.

All ye assembled in my sight,
Bow before my spirit bright.

Coveners bow before High Priestess.

Aphrodite, Arionhod,
Lover of the Horned God,
Mighty Queen of Witchery and night,
Morgan, Etoine, Nisene,
Diana, Bridgid, Melusine,
Am I named of old by men,
Artemis and Cerridwen,
Hell's dark mistress. Heaven's queen.
Ye who would ask of me a rune,
Or who would ask of me a boon,
Meet me in some secret glade,
Dance my round in greenwood shade,
By the light of the Full Moon.
In a place, wild and lone,
Dance my round in greenwood shade,

Dance about mine altar stone;
Work my holy mystery.
Ye who are feign to sorcery,
I bring ye secrets yet unknown.
No more shall ye know slavery,
Who give true worship unto me.
Ye who tread my round on Sabbat night,
Come ye all naked to the rite,
In token that ye be really free.
I teach ye the mystery of rebirth,
Work ye my mysteries in mirth.
Heart joined to heart and lip to lip,
Five are the points of fellowship,
That bring ye ecstasy on earth,
For I am the circle of rebirth.
I ask no sacrifice, but do bow,
No other Law but love I know,
By naught but love may I be known.
All things living are mine own,
From me they come, to me they go.

After effects of this ceremony are over, all should be purified in sacrifice before Her. She should then purify the High Priest and other men without partners with Her own hands. All partake of cakes and wine. Followed by feasting and singing, and dancing or fertility rites for good crops.

The Beltane Sabbat

The Summer Solstice

June 21

The Cauldron is wreathed with summer flowers and placed South of the Altar in the Magic Circle. A fire is built in it. The Magic Circle is cast and all are purified as usual.

The High Priestess assumes the God position while the High Priest, kneeling, invokes and draws down the Moon:

> *I invoke Thee and call upon Thee, O Mighty*
> *Mother of us all, Bringer of all Fruitfulness, by seed*
> *and by root, by stern and by bud, by leaf and flower*
> *and fruit, by life and by love do I invoke Thee to*
> *descend upon the body of Thy Servant and High*
> *Priestess,* (name).

All coveners concentrate while the High Priestess recites the Charge of the Goddess:

> *All ye assembled at mine shrine,*
> *Mother Darksome and Divine.*
> *Mine the Scourge and mine the Kiss,*
> *Here I charge you in this sign.*

Assumes Goddess position.

> *All ye assembled in my sight,*
> *Bow before my spirit bright.*

Coveners bow before High Priestess.

> *Aphrodite, Arionhod.*
> *Lover of the Horned God,*
> *Mighty Queen of Witchery and night,*
> *Morgan, Etoine, Nisene,*
> *Diana, Bridgid, Melusine,*
> *Am I named of old by men,*
> *Artemis and Cerridwen,*
> *Hell's dark mistress, Heaven's queen.*

Ye who would ask of me a rune,
Or who would ask of me a boon,
Meet in some secret glade,
Dance in my round in greenwood shade,
By the light of the Full Moon.
In a place, wild and lone
Dance about mine altar stone;
Work my holy mystery.
Ye who are feign to sorcery,
I bring ye secrets yet unknown.
No more shall ye know slavery,
Who give true worship unto me.
Ye who tread my round on Sabbat night,
Come ye all naked to the rite,
In token that ye be really free.
I teach ye the mystery of rebirth,
Work ye my mysteries in mirth.
Heart joined to heart and lip to lip,
Five are the points of fellowship,
That bring ye ecstasy on earth,
For I am the circle of rebirth.
I ask no sacrifice, but do bow,
No other Law but love I know,
By naught but love may I be known.
All things living are mine own,
From me they come, to me they go.

The High Priestess stands behind the Cauldron in the God position. The coveners file past, sunwise, alternately male-female. The men give her the sign of the 1, 2, 3 triangle and the Kiss of Fealty; the women bow to her. Then each takes a taper from the High Priest and lights it at the Cauldron. The High Priestess assumes the Goddess position, and the coveners walk slowly around the Magic Circle.

The High Priest recites:

> *Queen of the Moon,*
> *Queen of the Stars,*
> *Queen of the Horns,*
> *Queen of the Fires,*
> *Queen of the Earth,*
> *Bring to us the Child of Promise!*
> *For it is the Great Mother*
> *Who gives birth to Him;*
> *It is the Lord of Life*
> *Who is born again.*
> *Darkness and tears are set aside,*
> *When the Sun comes up again.*
> *Golden Sun of hill and mountain,*
> *Illumine the world,*
> *Illumine the Seas,*
> *Illumine the rivers,*
> *Illumine us all.*
> *Grief be laid and joy be raised,*
> *Blessed be the Great Mother!*
> *Without beginning, without end,*
> *Everlasting to Eternity.*
> *Evoe! Io! Evoe! He!*
> *Blessed Be! Blessed Be!*

The High Priest then leads the dance around the High Priestess and the Altar to the Circle Chant. All chant:

> *EKO EKO AZARAK,*
> *EKO EKO ZOMELEK,*
> *EKO EKO ARIDA,*
> *EKO EKO KERNUNNOS.*
> *BEZABI, LACHA, BACHABABA.*
> *LAMACH, CAHI, ACHABABA,*
> *KARRELOS, CAHI, ACHABABA,*

LAMACH LAMACH BACHAROUS,
CARBAHAJI, SABALYOS,
BARYLOS.
LAZOS, ATHAME, CALYOLAS,
SAMAHAC, ET FAMYOLAS,
HARRAHYA!

The High Priest gives the High Priestess the sign of the 1, 2, 3 triangle and the Kiss of Fealty. All men do likewise; the women bow.

After the ceremony there are cakes and wine, games and dancing.

The Lammas Sabbat

August 1

High Priestess or High Priest casts the Magic Circle. High Priestess at the Altar says:

> I (name) *High Priestess and Witch, do hereby invoke Thee O loving Arida, Mother of all things. As Thy Laws are, so shalt they be. Great is the Mother who has given us such tools as shall till the earth. Great is the Mother who has given us hands and a mouth for swallowing, who makest us grow without our knowledge and breathe whilst we are asleep.*

High Priestess salutes the four quarters. High Priestess says:

> *HEAR YE, O my people. The ploughland is heavy with the golden wheat of life, the cattle are bound, good substance fills the house, fair women are in their homes, and with just laws good men rule in wealth and prosperity. The boys go gladly with the girls in flowing dances and gambol and frolic in the turf's sweet flowers.*

Coveners reply:

> *We hear thee, O Great Mother, and give thanks.*

High Priest salutes to the four quarters. High Priestess salutes to the four quarters and says:

> *Hear ye, O my people, of the Power the Gods may give you. Remember this all those who have taken it upon themselves to have great powers, far greater than those of others, have incurred for a time hatred and unpopularity, but if one has to pursue a great aim this burden of envy must be accepted and it is wise to accept it. Hatred does not last forever, but the brilliance of the past is the glory of the future*

stored up in the memory of men. It is for you to
safeguard against hatred and cherish that future
glory and to do nothing now that is dishonorable.
But first you must purify your mind and your body,
saying to yourself, "Now it is my life I must shape as
a carpenter shapes wood and the thing to be formed
is a righteousness toward the Gods, as nothing is to
me the body, and as nothing the parts thereof." Let
death come when it will and I shall flee it not, for
now they shall cast you out of the Universe.
Wherever thou shall go there will be the Sun and
the Moon and the Stars and Vision and
Communion with the Gods.

Coveners reply:

We hear ye, O Great Mother, and seek purity.

The Witches are then given a kiss, anointed and then scourged.
The High Priestess is at the Altar chanting:

Mother of all things, come Thou beautiful one, Only
begotten Goddess of Light. Accept these offerings we
humbly give.

High Priest lights incense which Handmaiden hands to him.
Fruits are presented and offered up. Wine is presented and offered
up. Bread is presented and offered up.

High Priest says:

Hear, Blessed Goddess, we offer these fruits of the
Earth. Grant us in return abundant health and
prosperity and all the joys of life. Ye, as Queen of all
Delights, we ask.

High Priest and High Priestess lead dance around Altar with
phallic riding poles or broomsticks, with Circle Chant:

EKO EKO AZARAK,
EKO EKO ZOMELEK,

EKO EKO ARIDA,
EKO EKO KERNUNNOS,
BEZABI, LACHA, BACHABABA.
LAMACH, CAHI, ACHABABA,
KARRELOS, CAHI, ACHABABA,
KARRELOS, CAHI, ACHABABA,
LAMACH LAMACH BACHAROUS,
CARBAHAJI, SABALYOS,
BARYLOS.
LAZOS, ATHAME, CALYOLAS,
SAMAHAC, ET FAMYOLAS,
HARRAHYA!

All coveners partake of cakes and wine and feast and dancing. Great Rite.

The Samhain Sabbat

The Autumnal Equinox
September 21

The Altar should be decorated with symbols of autumn: pine cones, oak sprigs, acorns, ripe ears of corn and dried leaves, autumn flowers, etc.

High Priest forms the Magic Circle. High Priest enters the Circle with the High Priestess. High Priestess purifies High Priest who returns scourging. Male coveners purify the female witches and they scourge the men in return. High Priest stands at the West side of the Altar in the God position.

High Priestess stands at the East side of the Altar facing the High Priest. High Priestess says:

> *Farewell O Sun, ever returning light,*
> *The Hidden God who ever yet remains,*
> *Who now departs to the Land of Youth.*
> *Through the Gates of Death,*
> *To dwell enthroned, the judge of Gods and men.*
> *Horned leader of the Hosts of Air,*
> *Yet ever as He stands unseen about the Circle,*
> *So dwelleth He within the Sacred Seed,*
> *The seed of newly ripened grain.*
> *Hidden in earth, the seed of the Stars,*
> *In Him is life and life is the Light of Man.*
> *That which was never born, can never die,*
> *So the Wicca weep not but rejoice.*

High Priestess draws near to High Priest and with a kiss gives him the phallic-tipped riding pole or broomstick. High Priest leads the dance with High Priestess who holds the sistrum, the witches following around the Altar chanting the Invocation to the Horned God.

> *By the flame that burneth bright,*
> *O Horned One!*

We call Thy name into the night,
O Ancient One!
Thee we invoke, by the Moon-led sea,
By the standing stone and the twisted tree.
Thee we invoke, where gather Thine own,
By the nameless shore, forgotten and lone.
Come where the round of the dance is trod,
Horn and Hoof of the Goat Foot God!
By moonlit meadow, on dusky hill,
When the haunted wood is hushed and still,
Come to the charm of the chanted prayer,
As the Moon bewitches the midnight air.
Evoke Thy powers that potent bide,
In shining stream and the secret tide.
In fiery flame by starlight pale,
In shadowy host that rides the gale.
And by the ferndrakes, fairy haunted,
Of forests wild and woods enchanted,
Come? O Come!
To the heart-beat's drum!
Come to us who gather below,
When the broad white Moon is climbing slow.
Through the stars to the heavens' height,
We hear Thy hoofs on the wind of night!
As black tree branches shake and sigh,
By joy and terror we know Thee nigh.
We speak the spell Thy power unlocks,
At Solstice, Sabbat, and Equinox!

High Priestess and High Priest and the Handmaiden perform the Blessing of the Cakes and Wine. The High Priestess dismisses the spirits of the Watchtowers and closes the Circle.

Dancing—any form that pleases the entire group. If hungry— eat.

232   •   The Book of Shadows

The Hallowmas Sabbat

Halloween

October 31

All the coveners are properly prepared, naked and bound. All are purified by the Scourge. Prepare the place of worship. Place two black candles on the Altar. Place one red candle at the four corners (East, South, West, and North). A wreath of autumn flowers is on the Altar—the Crown of the Horned God is there also. The High Priest or the High Priestess forms the Magic Circle. Coveners enter the Circle. High Priest says:

> *O Gods, beloved of us all, Bless this our Sabbat that*
> *we, thy humble worshippers, may meet in love, joy,*
> *and bliss. Bless our rites this night with the presence*
> *of our departed kin.*

High Priest stands facing North with arms upraised and Sword held aloft. Coveners stand round him in semicircle holding hands. He then invokes the Horned God, saying:

> *By the flame that burneth bright,*
> *O Horned One!*
> *We call Thy name into the night,*
> *O Ancient One!*
> *Thee we invoke, by the Moon-led sea,*
> *By the standing stone and the twisted tree.*
> *Thee we invoke, where gather Thine own,*
> *By the nameless shore, forgotten and lone.*
> *Come where the round of the dance is trod,*
> *Horn and Hoof of the Goat Foot God!*
> *By moonlit meadow, on dusky hill,*
> *When the haunted wood is hushed and still,*
> *Come to the charm of the chanted prayer,*
> *As the Moon bewitches the midnight air.*
> *Evoke Thy powers that potent bide,*
> *In shining stream and the secret tide.*

In fiery flame by starlight pale,
In shadowy host that rides the gale.
And by the ferndrakes, fairy haunted,
Of forests wild and woods enchanted,
Come? O Come!
To the heart-beat's drum!
Come to us who gather below,
When the broad White Moon is climbing slow.
Through the stars to the heavens' height,
We hear Thy hoofs on the wind of night!
As black tree branches shake and sigh,
By joy and terror we know Thee nigh.
We speak the spell Thy power unlocks,
At Solstice, Sabbat, and Equinox!

High Priest leads the High Priestess and coveners in the meeting
dance. He with the riding pole held head upwards to represent the
phallus. Slow dance to the Witches' Chant:

Darksome night and shining Moon,
Hearken to the Witches' rune.
East then South, West then North,
Here! Come! I call Thee forth.
By all the powers of land and sea,
Be obedient unto me.
Wand and Pentacle and Sword,
Hearken ye unto my word.
Cords and Censer. Scourge and Knife,
Waken all ye into life.
Powers of the Witches' Blade,
Come ye as the charge is made.
Queen of Heaven, Queen of Hell,
Send your aid unto the spell.
Horned Hunter of the night,
Work my will by magic rite.
By all the powers of land and sea,

As I do say, "So mote it be."
By all the might of Moon and Sun,
As I do will, it shall be done.

The High Priest and High Priestess invoke again. High Priestess says:

Dread Lord of the Shadows, God of Life and Bringer
of Death. Yet as the knowledge of Thee is Death,
Open wide, I pray Thee, Thy gates through which
all must pass. Let our dear ones, who have gone
before, return this night to make merry with us.
And when our time comes, as it must, O Thou, the
Comforter and Consoler, The Giver of Peace and
Rest, we will enter Thy realm gladly and unafraid.
For we know that when rested and refreshed among
our dear ones, we will be reborn again by Thy grace
and that of the Lady Arida. Let it be the same place
and same time as our dear ones, that we may love
again. O Horned One, descend, we pray, on (name
High Priest), *Thy High Priest and Witch.*

High Priestess goes to High Priest and with pine-tipped Wand, draws an invoking Pentagram on his chest and on a wreath of autumn flowers on the Altar. High Priest kneels and High Priestess places ring (crown) of flowers on his head. Each witch is given a red taper lit from the candles on the Altar and large quantities of incense are scattered on the censer's burning ashes. High Priestess strikes the bell forty times with her Athame and says:

Hear Ye, my Witches,
Welcome to our Great Sabbat.
Welcome we the Spirits
Of our departed kin.

High Priestess strikes forty times on the bell again. Witches walk slowly around the Circle. High Priestess fills the Cup with wine and hands it to High Priest who drinks.

High Priest:

> *In humility, as the Horned One asks, I bid my*
> *Witches drink.*

High Priest takes the Cup to the first witch, giving it with the right hand whilst taking the taper with left and extinguishing it. This is repeated with each witch.

High Priest says:

> *Listen, my Witches, to the words of the Horned One.*
> *Drink, dance, and be merry in the presence of the*
> *Old Gods and the Spirits of our departed kin.*

Coveners partake of the cakes and wine. Dances and games may be enjoyed by all. The Great Rite. Close the Circle. Merry Meet, Merry Part.

Appendix

An Old Sabbat Rite

An Old Solitary Midnight Candlemas

Be ye properly prepared. Bless thyself with Earth, Fire, Wind, and Water exactly at midnight.

Kindle your fire; it does not have to be beneath a Cauldron. If you have nothing else, use a candle flame; or you may tie a bundle of faggots together or use a bundle of pine splinters tied together. In today's world a cigarette lighter will do, if you have no other source of fire. Stand before the flame in the Pentagram position. Now invoke your Deity, saying:

> *Ancient of ancients,*
> *rayed in beauty,*
> *Horny with power*
> *Hurry to me.*
> *Without Thy light and warmth*
> *I shall surely die.*
> *'Tis Candlemas and I await Thee.*
> *Warm the sleeping seed within the belly*
> *of our Earth Mother.*
> *Quicken and comfort me,*
> *Renew my strength.*
> *Look, I have kindled a fire of welcome.*
> *My fire burns brightly.*
> *Sustain my Horn of Power*
> *in a mighty erection.*

> *I do faithfully serve Thee.*
> *Hasten and warm*
> *My cold and frozen land.*
> *I bid Thee welcome.*

Rest and meditate until the dawning of morning light. Stroke thy fire. Light thy torch. The Ancient One returneth. His horns rise out of the sea. His fiery flame burns on the far horizon. Stand and bid him welcome!

Comment: It is not always possible to be with a Coven or with others at Candlemas time, but the Ancient Rites must be kept.

I hope that you will find joy in this lovely ritual, even though it does seem to be especially for males. I am sure you ladies could adapt it very nicely. My adaptation reads:

> *I have kindled a fire of welcome,*
> *My fire burns brightly.*
> *Sustain my fiery Cauldron*
> *Upon Thy Horn of Power.*
> *Seduce me with Thy mighty erection.*
> *I am Thine and Thou art mine.*
> *Hasten unto me;*
> *Keep me unto Thyself.*
> *Love me as no other can,*
> *For I am Thine alone.*

Designed and typeset by Connie Hill
in Trajan and Minion typefaces. Trajan, a classic font designed by
Carol Twombly, is based on the lettering on Trajan's Column in Rome.
Minion is a contemporary typeface designed by Robert Slimbach.

Printed by Friesens at Altona, Manitoba, on Miami Hi-bulk, a fine-
quality recycled paper